"It's not often you meet people like Paul and Julia. Paul is an ideas machine and Julia has a stack of marketing knowledge unlike anyone else. Here you have guys that always wants to go the extra mile to help your business prosper and keep you well on track. They have a refreshing approach that never fails to deliver."
Adam Cliff - *Co- Founder, Make it Media*

"Julia is a power house of ideas and inspiration. She is brilliant keeping you on your toes, and holding you accountable, she has huge amounts of bubbly personality that is contagious, you will learn heaps form her and in turn earn more just from knowing her! Hire Julia you won't regret it!"
Thomas Bower - *Owner & Head Honcho, Thomas the Caterer*

"I had a business idea about eight years ago. For eight years I had been trying to market it, mostly without success and even though I was sure it could work, I had pretty much given up.
Yesterday I sat down with Paul and within two hours he had given me an unbelievably clear idea of what I needed to do. This was not some one-plan-fits-all approach: Paul paid great attention to my idea, saw immediately what was relevant (and what was not) and drew up a precise and achievable marketing strategy. For eight years I had been walking under a cloud of marketing confusion. Two hours with Paul, and the sun is finally shining."
Rob Glass - *Owner, Coracle Films*

"It's really simple. I just did what Julia and Paul told me to do. I used the tools they gave me, I made £6000 and I've created a new subscription income."
Jackie Crooks - *Owner, Beacon Training*

"Uninterrupted 1:1 focus session last Tuesday morning with Paul Chapman . Really got me fired up and we got a stack of stuff done that I've been meaning to do for ages. The session has resulted in 18k's worth of new sales thus far."
Peter Caswell - *CEO, Orbit Pharmaceutical*

"I wouldn't be without the Marketing Jumpleads Library. It gives me the tools I need and the accountability to focus on what I should be doing to grow my business. What i have learnt has brought us several large new clients on board recently plus a stack of smaller ones too. It's a great way to learn how to market your business without being overwhelmed."
Tina Clarke - *Co-Owner, Cube Upholstery*

THE GAME CHANGERS

37 STRATEGIES TO HELP YOU ACHIEVE THE BUSINESS YOU WANT.

Paul Chapman and Julia Roberts

About the authors Paul and Julia

Paul Chapman and Julia Roberts are two of the UK's favourite Business Experts and have worked with over 600 business owners in the last 4 years.

Straight talking, practical and full of ideas the two of them make a formidable team, who cut through the fluff and theories and offer real-world solutions to find and keep customers for your business.

Running a business takes grit. It's also exciting. It's your freedom. Your livelihood. Your dreams,

Paul and Julia created Marketing Jumpleads, to help business owners grow, without feeling overwhelmed because it's tough on your own. Jumpleads provides help, up-to-date strategies and a supportive, smart, business community.

Speaking, training and running national marketing campaigns they live and breathe all things marketing. This book shares their best insights and encourages you to TAKE ACTION.

Please get in touch if you have any questions or we can help in any way.

www.marketingjumpleads.com   www.marketingjumpleads.nz

+44 (0)116 4300103

Copyright © 2016 Paul Chapman and Julia Roberts
Design by Clare McCabe
All rights reserved.
ISBN-13: 978-1539880028
ISBN-10: 1539880028
Second Edition

Dedication

A huge thank you to our families & friends for their love and support and who have put up with our long working hours, waffling idea dumps and single minded passion working on our business.

To our clients who inspire us every day.

Game changer contents

Introduction

We simply love running our business. We run several and help many more. We thrive on the opportunity and enormous privilege being an entrepreneur, at this time in history, brings. But it's not always easy.

The route to success is a roller coaster of highs and lows. It can even feel lonely at times. Entrepreneurship is a constant path of learning, testing, tweaking and then amplifying what works. A journey of champagne highs and sleepless nights, that we'd never swap.

The Game Changers shares our experiences over 40+ combined years in business. As geeky marketing bods we share our most successful marketing ideas, plus our best overarching business thinking and techniques that will get your business moving. Game changing insights.

We believe there is no 'silver bullet' to business success. No 'get rich' fad that you can copy and become an overnight millionaire. There is however a smart way of thinking, an approach to your business that can change everything.

Many of the ideas in this book will challenge you. Some may even directly oppose what you believe to be true. What we can say over the 15+ years mentoring growing businesses, the strategies here are tried and tested.

We strongly encourage you to study them carefully, put them into practice and judge the results for yourself.

We've worked with some incredible people over the years and admired others. As a book bonus we're also sharing interviews with some of them. These insights from successful entrepreneurs, who are working in their business day-in-day-out, just like you, are pure gold dust.

We want to thank them for sharing their magic of thinking big, believing anything is possible and confiding in how they make their business work.

Read about their journey. Discover the business strategies that keep them successful and inspired...and importantly adopt some of them.

Before you start...

Before you go about any marketing or business changes you need to be sure that what you're doing leads to where you want to be. Start by asking one big question. Be careful here as it would be easy to dismiss this as fluffy nonsense, but the truth is this could be the biggest question you have ever asked yourself.

What do you want your life to be like?

We have met so many business owners who, if they won the lottery, would pack it all in, because they don't really enjoy what they do.

That is really sad. They spend so much time doing something they don't enjoy and making their business a success becomes very hard, if not impossible.

Running a business means that you have a choice about everything: how much you earn; who you work with; how much you work and especially what activities fill each day.

This has to be where you start. What do you want to spend your day doing? What are you best at? Are you spending your time wisely?

The point here is that it isn't any harder to produce a residual income each month, leaving you free to do other things, than it is to sell your time for money per hour – but the steps and thus marketing that needs to take place will be very different.

Success for all of us is measured in very different ways. You'll read in the business owners interviews that the 'millionaire' dream is NOT what most of us want. It's often about family time, having control and defining and shaping our own working life.

But you have to start with that clarity.

What do you want YOUR life to be like? We meet so many business owners who are wholly reactive. Julia would say she spent way too many years as a 'busy fool' juggling the day to day of her beauty business, without any real plan, clarity or control of her time.

This book has been written to help you choose what you do with your tomorrow.

Amidst the doom and gloom and media scaremongering about the economy and business we love this quote, from Marc Wileman, Sublime Science which you'll find later in the book...

"I think so many people seem to have lost sight of the fact this is the most abundant time ever. We've got more tools and technology at our disposal than ever before....What we do have is absolutely phenomenal"

Marketing is not a secret science. You need neither a degree, an affiliation to a governing body or a special talent. It's not magic and it's not a silver bullet. It's not easy but neither is it difficult. And the good news is that there is genuinely no failure with marketing. It is a series of tests, some activities will bring results – others won't work – and some of the things that you have tried before will get a different result when tweaked and re-tried – that's the game.

But the good news is any business will only EVER need 3 things to get new clients:

- The right person to talk to
- The right thing to tell them
- The right way to link the two

In that order!

The key here is the word RIGHT – not all the people you will talk to are the right people for your business. Some won't want what you have and some will never pay what you want to charge for it. But enough people will.

Because people have different worries, agendas, needs and aspirations they will need to be told something that is relevant to them and their lives and thought processes – if you try and attract them with a bland message that could be written for anyone you will disappear into the noise.

Once you have worked these bits out it gets a lot easier.

This book comes with a host of bonus materials, which will help you define your right audience and message to them. You'll find it all here:
www.marketingjumpleads.com/game-changer-book-bonuses

Our biggest game changing tip...Take action. Marketing and activity is critical to all business, without it you simply cannot grow, so get into the book, think about the ideas but most importantly try them.

REWARDS ARE FOR THOSE WHO TAKE ACTION.

Take action

Julia and Paul.

Become an entrepreneur, not a business owner

Become an entrepreneur, not a business owner

There is a big difference between being a business owner and an entrepreneur. Most people think these terms are interchangeable but they're not.

And most often it comes down to the way someone thinks and what they will "settle' for in terms of success for their business.

Most business owners essentially have a job. Their actions and lifestyles are dictated by their business needs whereas entrepreneurs have a business in order to facilitate their lifestyle.

This might sound derogatory to business owners, but it isn't meant to be. They are doing something the overwhelming majority of the population will never be able to do. But the reality of the situation is that most business owners do not have the freedom they set out to achieve. Often the difference is that the Entrepreneur has "considered their business consciously."

They have looked at it and thought *"what's the point of doing this?" "What do I want my business to do for me and my family?"*

They then look at how they can direct their business to achieve those results for themselves.

The truth is that it is no harder to set up a business that can run successfully without the owner being physically there full-time, than it is to run a business that demands them as the linchpin every day. However they will need to be conscious that that is the aim of it all and be willing to undertake the activities needed to achieve this – which will be different from what is considered the "norm."

To the entrepreneur their business is a tool to get them where they want to get to, if the tool is working - if it's the wrong tool they will make changes because for them the result is far more important that the method of getting there.

So where do you sit, do you own the business or does the business own you?

The good news is wherever you are now it is genuinely never too late to make that change. The world (and your local business community) is covered with examples of people doing just that, as one Marketing Jumpleads member put it...

"I just woke up – I still love my business but I now see it as a means to an end not the all encompassing "master" it was. I use it to fund my lifestyle which it is now doing 3 times better than it was before. I just look at it differently and that really helps me to make clear decisions"

Chris started brokenStones over 20 years ago with one simple aim: To make IT easier for businesses.
Today he has a large team providing IT support and consultancy services to businesses across the UK. Operating out of their HQ in Lichfield and recently opened 2nd office in Wales they provide both remote and onsite support as well as supplying a whole range of hardware and software.
He's a genuinely nice guy who's always happy to help...
http://brokenstones.co.uk/

Paul: So lets kick off with an easy one. What is it really about for you? Why are you doing this? Why are you running a business as opposed to, say, having a job?

Chris: Freedom, I guess, is one thing. Although, I don't feel like freedom is the important thing to me. But I think I'd miss it a lot if it was not there. Having said that, I do work an awful lot more than I'd done if I had "a normal job."

But I've always been someone who has worked hard at whatever I've done and I kind of see it as, when I used a normal job, I put in well above and beyond what is normally expected. And, really, why should I do that for someone else when I can do it for myself and do better for myself. Lots of people say that it's about their family and about this, that, and the other.

And I get that, and I get that feeling sometimes. But, deep down, I don't feel like it is about that for me. It is about the excitement and being in control of your own future really.

Paul: So on that then, what does success look like to you? I don't think the phrase "made it" really applies to guys like us, but when you sit back in five, ten years, you're looking back, how will you know you've done what you wanted to do with the tools that you've got i.e. your business?

Chris: It'll be because I'll know I can do whatever I want to do. I am quite a materialistic person and things like nice cars, a nice house, nice holidays are important to me. I've been able to afford the things that I want to get. It is very prominent on my goal list, on my life achievement list, to own a Ferrari or two. I'd like to be able to just jump in that and go for a little spin. And, equally, having then the freedom, if I wake up one morning and think, you know what, I fancy having a good game of golf today. Success to me is sort of having the freedom to be able to choose what I do without limits really.

Paul: I think, mate, whether you'd admit it yourself, by any stretch of the imagination, you've done really well. You've built a great business today. Why do you think that is? Why do you think you have done well?

Chris: I suppose the first thing is I don't feel like I'm there yet. Up until very recently, I've always felt like I've been a long way away from that. And I can't quite put my finger on what's happened recently, but I've become more in tune with it, where I am now, and the things I have, and the choices I can make. And I do kind of feel like I am well on my way now. I feel a lot more comfortable over where I'm going and kind of where I am getting to now.

I don't think it is any specific actions that I've done. I think it's sort of a change of mindset really. I think because you are in it – it's sort of hard to see but when you talk to other people who are where you have been , and then explaining the things you've done in terms of moving your business forward and they are no where near that level of action or even thinking reminds me of how far we have come. As an example, over the weekend, talking to another IT guy who is probably four, five years behind where I am now. And he was asking me questions about how I'd solved this problem or what I've done to overcome this sort of challenge. Just kind of talking through with him, and I could tell him other things I've changed in the business, the systems which we've put in place. That's what's kind of made me feel like, oh, I'm sort of getting somewhere now really.

Paul: Is there anything that you think has got you to where you are? Is it your mindset? Or do you think a lot of it is just time? The longer you have been doing it the more you have succeeded?

Chris: I don't know whether it is time because I have seen people who have then got there quickly. And I don't know whether it is the whole mindset thing. I mean, certainly, I would say it is something I have changed a lot over the last three or four years, that has helped me move forwards a lot quicker. A big thing has been having mentors around me. I have worked with several mentors, who have then helped me develop my thinking really, just kind of get me to think about things different. And I often think, if I'd had that support right back at day one, that would have helped me move along a hell of a lot quicker right back at the start.

Paul: Yeah, I think that's something that a lot of businesses need, but actually they try and do it all themselves at the beginning for cash flow reasons which I do understand but I think it is a real false economy. Actually, having someone in your corner as early as you can just stop so many of the mistakes and wasting time and money on things that won't work or just aren't important.

Chris: Especially with what I do and my kind of background with that, that techie sort of background, we naturally think that we are the best at something and as such why do we need external help because we can do it all by ourself? And that is probably a big change which has then taken place over the years. For me it was a realisation that actually having someone else to put a different view on things is a good thing. And I should not be defensive about it, and not be afraid that someone else does actually know more than me, and I can learn things from them, learn from other people's experiences.

Paul: Leading on from that, why do you think most business owners struggle or fail? I don't mean that in a judgmental way. But, I think, in our circle in particular, we look at businesses around us and you can see those that if you're brutally honest, aren't going to make it. Why do you think it is? What is that difference?

Chris: Certainly, the ones which I see which are struggling, are the one's with "big barriers up". When you try and give them a bit of advice or tips or sort of benefits of your own experience, and there's a very common answer that they come back with, which is the whole "Yes, but..." "Yes, but I'm different." "Yes, but that won't work for me because this" and have a very closed mind there is nothing that is going to work for them because they are different. Whereas, I like to take the approach now of looking at how can I make that work for me?

Paul: Yes we do see that a lot, I do think in business there is very little that is new, the methods change a bit but the fundamentals are the same and it always frustrates us when someone only see's the 'black and white' of a solution rather than the concept of it. It does stagger me, when people can't let their guard down as a business owner. The best most successful business owners learn from anything there is always someone else's business can show them, even if it's just how not to do something.

So following on from that, is there one thing that you look back and you wish you'd known when you had started? Something you wished you known or done or wish you had avoided?

I suppose, if I was to start all over again now and not know the things I know now, the one thing which I really could have done with then is someone telling me that the single most important thing I can do to help me develop my business is to have a mentor right from day one.

Paul: If you did it all over again, is that the thing you'd do differently?

Chris: Yes. I would have someone else sat on my shoulder putting an external perspective on things for me. And I would not be afraid to take their advice, or to listen, or to consider what they're saying, as opposed to dismiss it as thinking I know better.

Paul: It is crucial to have that outside kind of pair of ears, pair of eyes. It's so hard to see what is really going on in your own business when you are on the inside. But, notwithstanding having someone else in your corner, can you point at one strategy, something that you have employed in your business that has been your most potent.

Chris: That's a deep-thinking question, that one is. Isn't it?

Paul: I do what I can.

Chris: It's quite hard to think of something straight off. There's been lots of little things which I've done.

Paul: Tell us about those.

Chris: It's simple things like realising you can't get everything done on your to-do list. So, rather than sit and work out what you can and can't get done, rather than sit and work out what's important, just sit down and just pick one thing. Get that done and move on to the next one because, at the end of the day, you find out you've got a hell of a lot more done than if you'd sat and thought about what was important to do. Something that I've been doing more of lately and which has helped me move forward faster lately has been doing a lot more reading as well, so reading a lot more books, learning a lot more from those books. And I guess I realised that I went to school, I did my A-levels, I went to university, and then my learning kind of stopped. And it was only again in recent years I've realised just how daft that was really, and actually how you should be proactively trying to keep learning improving.

You know I like to play tennis. I like my tennis. And I have a lot of lessons and different coaching sessions. And other people often say to me, "Are you still having lessons? Are you still not good enough?" And I just talk about Andy Murray or Roger Federer. They haven't stop learning and they haven't stopped having a coach, do they? And they're at the very top of the game."

Paul: As the closing out, if there were a bunch of business owners sitting in front of you, what would you tell them? They've kind of got all the basics there, they have all the building blocks, they're just in that rabbit-in-the-headlights moment. What would be your big bit of advice?

Chris: Again, I think it comes back down to having a mentor, having a coach, because they can look at things externally for you, give you the guidance, so help to point you in the right direction because they're not wrapped up in the day-to-day and they're not blinded by all these million and one things you have around you. Trusting what they see from an external perspective they can help guide you on that one thing that is important for you. Because I think it is different for all people. We all come from different backgrounds, we've got different skills. I've got a very good technical, problem-solving skill set there and, so, I can solve logical problems and I can kind of think outside the box fairly easily. Whereas, you see other people struggle with that. Whereas, things like the accountancy side of things, and knowing my numbers, I was a bit slower to pick up on that. And, so, having someone externally who can then help guide you in the right direction, so I think it's different for everyone really.

I would add, if there was some silver bullet, then surely that's what everyone would be doing. Whereas, because it is different for everyone, something which has worked for one person does not necessarily work for the next. You need to find out what the thing is for you really. What do you do best – do more of that. And what has helped me in recent times is then having someone there to point that out really, and to slap me when you're not doing it, and to then highlight what you should be focused on.

Game Changer Two

Build
a tribe

Build a tribe

There is no substitute for building and nurturing a list of people who have an interest in what you do.

Without the ability to easily talk to people who you KNOW are at least passively interested in the product or service you sell, you will always struggle to consistently grow your business and it will always feel like you are trying to push water up hill.

Having a list of people that you can speak to when you need to is like having the ability to turn a tap on for your business.

It's more than a game changer, it's a life changer. It means that you are in control of the selling conversation

It doesn't just happen and it isn't about accumulating lists of 1000's of people. We would rather take 100 of the right people than 10,000 any bodies. That will just sap your time and waste your money.

Building you list should be one of your business key day-to-day activities and there are loads of ways to do it.

Past clients
People you meet at shows
People you meet networking
Forums
Social media channels
Online lead baits
Competitions
Selling something different

Whenever you come across somebody that shows an interest, (whether it be online or offline), grab their details and send or offer them something useful ... and then keep doing it.

Treat them nicely, don't always sell to them, but keep in regular contact with things that are helpful and relevant. They will be drawn closer to you and you will be seen as the expert, so when you do send them an opportunity to buy they will be far more likely to do so and be happier with their decision.

One Marketing Jumpleads member did just this and made £170,000 in 6 weeks without finding any new clients.

Selling stuff is important – having a list is CRITICAL.

Book bonus available here:
www.marketingjumpleads.com/game-changer-book-bonuses

Game Changer Three

Be different - do It differently

Be different - do it differently

This strategy is KEY. If nothing else from this book take away this learning. On its own this level of thinking could explode your profits and raise your business high above your competitors.

 As Steve Jobs said "Here's to the crazy ones. The misfits. The rebels. The trouble-makers. The round pegs in the square holes. The ones who see things differently...they change things. They push the human race forward. And while some may see them as the crazy ones, we see genius"

This can apply to pretty much anything in life, but it can be MASSIVE when you adopt this thinking in your marketing. In most sectors there is the 'normal' way of marketing. Every solicitors firm, every beauty salon, every surveyor sees what everyone else in their industry is doing to win business and copies it! DO THE OPPOSITE TO EVERYONE ELSE.

We know this may seem scary or too hard. But we promise it will be a game changing strategy. Most business marketing is at best stagnated. Look at your current marketing and truthfully ask if it is working. If you need new ways to attract clients think 'outside the box' and leave the 'how its done around here' mentality behind.

Being bland and 'in the middle' will not win you the prizes. How many businesses in your sector, that you may be replicating, are flying high? If you want different results to your competitors you simply have to do things differently to them.

Look at what works in different sectors. What could you adopt for your business? Good marketeers will always be on the lookout for new ideas and thinking 'how can I make that work in my business?' The swipe file strategy will help you collect those good ideas.

This book will give you lots of tactics to help elevate and differentiate your marketing. You simply need to do what most of your competitors won't know or won't do.

Book bonus available here:
www.marketingjumpleads.com/game-changer-book-bonuses

Game Changer Four

It's a journey

It's a journey
- with bonus of full Customer Journey Course

Selling your products and services is a journey you must take with your potential new customers.

So at the very beginning...these people are complete strangers and you need to get to know them and vice versa. In a world where we are bombarded with thousands of marketing each day it's more important than ever than to really 'make friends' with these strangers and through a series of stages help them discover your products and services, not just go 'straight for the sale'. If you gently build your credibility and 'friendship' with them, some will go on to become true fan evangelists of your business.

REALLY understanding this full journey will distinguish your business from your competitors and you'll be able to fully release the true potential of your business profits.

Many business owners think that marketing almost exclusively is for finding new customers and getting them to buy the main service or product. WRONG!

The initial searching for strangers and making them aware of your business is JUST THE BEGINNING of the marketing journey.

Importantly the main profits, growth and sustainability of your business lies in successfully keeping existing customers excited about your products and services and keeping them spending continuously, whilst raving about your business to others.

This move from stranger to fan evangelist will involve you putting into place a fully-rounded journey where you hold the hand of your prospect and lead them through.

Our bonus work sheets and video will unveil the overall marketing picture and let you identify where you have gaps and where you should be focussing your efforts and money right now.

You can't do it all straight away...nor should you try. In time you will complete and fine-tune a full customer marketing journey so that you create a perpetual system for attracting, selling to, exciting and keeping long-term clients.

We firmly believe in working without continual overwhelm. You will see and hear about all kinds of funky marketing tactics but on their own they really don't help you. They have to be part of the full journey, each phase working hard to move your customers to the next phase in your relationship. This joined-up marketing journey that can then sit in your business (with some tweaks!) for years supporting customers and growing your profits.

Building this pathway properly and methodically will seriously unlock life-changing profits, which you'll soon discover lie in the hands of understanding this journey and leading customers to become repeat buyers and happy fans.

Book Bonus available here:
It's so important and fundamental to your marketing successwe're including our full
Customer Marketing Journey Course
www.marketingjumpleads.com/game-changer-book-bonuses

Ross Davies *StrafeCreative*

Ross Davies is a results-driven, creative and technically minded professional who works with Managing Directors and Marketing Directors to increase the number of leads that come from their websites.
He is currently the Managing Director for Strafe Creative, a design company with a conscience. His progressive Program/Project Management experience in Web Design, Graphic Design, Print Design, 3D Games Design, Product Development, & Information Technology has helped Strafe Creative become one of the fastest growing digital design agencies in Nottingham.

http://www.strafecreative.co.uk/
http://uk.linkedin.com/in/rossdavies

Paul: Let's get the ball rolling, what's it really about for you? Why do you run Strafe as opposed to, I don't know, having a job?

Ross: So, we honestly believe that design can transform a business. So, how you appear to the public, people's perceptions of you will make a dramatic difference to the number of sales you get, how many people want to interact with you. We genuinely believe that. And that's our main focus at all points, to make sure our clients look perfect for their target market. And having that as our starting point makes everything a little bit easier to know where we're going. That's kind of what gets us up in the morning. It means that I'm not necessarily focusing on getting as many sales. I'm not focusing on making as much money as possible. We're focusing on delivering great design. And then, off the back of that, that's where we get everything else. That's where we get other people wanting to work with us because that's our kind of main aim, that's our belief.

Paul: And do you think you couldn't do that in a job?

Ross: Obviously, we've all had jobs at other places, and what I like, or one of the main reasons about owning my own business rather than working for someone else is I can pick and choose what we do.

If I don't want to work with a client, we'll either price ourselves out of it, or we just won't take it on. So I think you don't get that in other businesses. And it's not even necessarily about the type of business, it's more the person that you're dealing with, that when you work at other jobs, you'll be forced to work with clients that you hate, or you might have managers that you hate. And you don't have to work -- you don't have to deal with that as a self-employed person. If you don't want to work with them, don't work with them. It's as simple as that. So we're less bothered about the company we work with. It's more the person that we'll be interacting with. I have no bones about working within different industries.

Paul: From a more personal point of view because I'm guessing that your business is your driver to deliver your lifestyle, what does success look like? How do you know when you've done what you want to do?

Ross: So we have our plans. We have one-year plans, three-year plans, and five-year plans of where we want to be. So I guess success, for me, is always hitting those targets, making sure we're going towards those goals. And, that's one of the main things I'd say when I look at what we've done compared to other design agencies, we've already got that plan in place, we know where we want to be, we know what we need to do to get there. And we've tried to think of the steps that are going to get us there. So do we need to employ more staff? We've got a full organisational chart so we know when people are going to come in, what time they're going to come in, what type of work we want to be doing. And, obviously, I think having that makes it a little bit easier to know kind of where we're going. Yeah.

Paul: So, I don't want to put you on the spot, why do you think you guys have done so well?

Ross: Good question. I think people like our approach, and they like our honesty. I think they believe that we're there to improve their business rather than let's just try to get a sale.

Paul: So do you think perhaps your successes come from the fact you have a higher purpose rather than are trying to sell a thing? So people like your ethos rather than what you deliver. Does that make sense?

Ross: Yeah, there's the book -- isn't it Your Why by Simon Sinek? And I think that story makes a big difference to us. We feel that that's important. Again, I kind of talk about the plan of where we're going and we're very self-aware of the market we're in. So we're aware of how we're positioned is important. So we enter lots of awards of and, luckily, we win a lot of awards as well. That type of thing makes a difference. We are aware that, obviously with what we're in, the web market, there's more and more bits of software that can kind of build it for you.

So we've kind of steered away from that bit of market, and then we focus a lot on conversion work, which isn't as popular at the moment. It's become a lot more popular in the past six months. But, I'd probably say, in Nottingham especially, there's only one or two of us really who are doing that. So I think it's just that kind of self-awareness and that it kind of comes back to this plan that we know where we want to be, we know how much, and that's kind of what we believe that success is, is if I hit all our targets and it gets to that point, then I know I'm successful. And I think a driven person will never be 100% happy because, otherwise, they'd settle. And I can't see myself being like, "Oh, I've got to 20 members of staff, I'm done." I'd be like, "Right, what's the next step? Where do we go now?" That's kind of how I see it.

Paul: So, conversely, why do you think most business owners struggle or fail?

Ross: They don't put in the time.

Paul: Yeah? Simple as?

Ross: They don't put in the time, they don't put in the effort, or they focus on the wrong things, I personally think. And we've made those mistakes as well. I remember when we first ste up and we were live, "It'll be live, right? We'll get our site live, and the work will just flood in."

Paul: I remember it well.

Ross: "People will just Google us, and we will make money." And it's not that. If people have a bad sales month, they're like, "Nothing's happening. "Well, did you cold call? Did you ring people up? Did you do an email campaign? Did you ring all of your current clients and ask them if they wanted any new services? Did you produce something that sold them on another service they might not know about? There's all these other things that people don't do. They just kind of go, "Oh, I've had a bad month." And I think it's too easy to make excuses. I think that's one of our main things, especially I take a lot of pride in our business. And I feel like if I've had a bad sales month, it's on us. We're the reason. There's no other reason why. It's not because, "Oh, this other version is cheaper" or this sort of thing. If we lose something on price, for example, this is very much a mentality thing. I don't see it as we've lost something on price because the other person was cheaper, I see it as we didn't get across our expertise and our value well enough. I think having that mentality is what separates you. Otherwise, it's too easy to blame other things and you give up. That's why I think people just don't put in the work.

Paul: Yeah, I think you're right. A lot of the people that we know of, they just talk a brilliant game, they'd like more money or more time off, but they are never willing to do the work, make the changes, to make it happen.

But I think a big thing about our business, at the moment, is there's too many. There's too many web guys, marketing guys, accountants, plumbers.

All the power is with the buyer so you've got to work harder to get a better message out.

Ross: Yeah. We are looking for a cabinet maker at the moment to come in and make some these sort of cabinets near the side of our fireplace. You'd think that would be a relatively easy thing to find. I can't find anyone on Google, can't find any recommendations, even checked the yellow pages, and people don't pick up the phone. I found one person as I was driving past. I saw a sign. So, even the fact that I have no credibility, no testimonial on this business, I thought, "I'm just going to pull in," and they weren't open. It was a weekend. I was just like, "Surely this would be prime time for people to want to come in and look at stuff that you've made." And these would be the people that are like, "Oh, I can't get any work in." It's like I can't physically find anyone to do this work in my area.

The truth is loads of people focus on totally the wrong thing, they kid themselves that they are doing stuff but it's the wrong stuff, it's not the stuff that makes them money.

Paul: I think, often, it comes to having an outside pair of eyes on your business as well because we've all been there. I think both you and I have been lucky to have people - well, not lucky, we've sought out people in the background to say, "Paul, why are you doing that?"

Ross: That's really important. In Think and Grow Rich by Napolean Hill he talks, obviously, about the mastermind mentality of how it's good to have that time out of your day when you aren't focusing on the business, but you're discussing it with other people. There will be things that people will just point out, saying, "Why don't you do that? Why don't you do this?" It's, "Ah." That's something that we've done for at least four or five years and that's really helpful to us. And it's what I try to do monthly.

Paul: I guess on that, what would be your biggest bit of advice to another business owner then?

Ross: It's something that took us a long time and actually, when we first set up, everyone was like, "Oh, make sure you do your business goals, and make sure you have the aim of where you want to be." But, actually, it's kind of a standard one, because your main focus becomes that, all of a sudden, makes it dead easy. So, if I said, for example, my goal was to make 100 websites at £1000 a pop, let's just say -- that's a terrible goal, but lets's go with it... That also means I know exactly what my target market is. I know exactly who I'm selling to. They'll be start-ups that only have a small amount of money. If I only want to sell 100 of them, there'll be a set way that I can do that. And that'll get me up in the morning. Whereas, if I just get up every day and go, "Oh, I'm going to build some websites," then where do I start? What do I do with that? Whereas, if it's build websites for startups at £1000 a pop, I'll build 100 of them, and I'll only work in Nottingham with people under 25, then that makes it easier. So I think knowing what you want to achieve from it makes it easier to do that. Otherwise, you're just swimming in a circle.

Paul: What do you think has been your most potent strategy, the thing that you've employed that's made the biggest difference to your success?

Ross: Experimenting. We try something at least once a month. We have weekly meetings, and we'll discuss ideas in those meetings. It might be that we'll have a marketing idea, or we might have something that will improve a process, or we might have a script that we didn't discuss that would make development easier. We'll just try it, so we'll invest time into doing it. And, if it works, it works. If it doesn't, we move on. But at least we're constantly trying stuff, and we're constantly trying new avenues. I think the worry is there's too many people who just get stuck in their ways and don't change, don't think of doing anything different. And, I mean, we've had some where we've lost a lot of money trying different ideas. But we've had little ones that made a load of money. And then, once you know the idea, you can then spend more money in it to make it even better. But then the more we try new things -- and I think just be willing to throw yourself in the deep end and try something new is important too.

Paul: If you could do it all again, what would you do differently?

Ross: I think, like I said, I'd get my plan in order quicker. It took us a while to learn that we needed a plan rather than just, "We'll set up a business, and people will give me money."

And then, "Well, how are you going to do that?" "People will find us." It's like there's just no thought process behind it. And it should be relatively obvious, but it isn't. You just don't think it's real. So I think planning is probably one of the main things that I'd do earlier. Or I'd do from the start.

Paul: And that perhaps answers the last question. Do you think that's the single biggest thing that's made the difference to your business, having that?

Ross: That's a really tough question. Yeah, I mean, there's lots of different things that could potentially come into it. But I think that one's important with everything. So, even before we start any project, before we start any marketing, if we've got the planning, we know where we want it to go, everything is easier. Whereas, we probably spent the first year, year and a half going, "Hey, we should try that," and not thinking anything through, and that just dilutes your effort and then the results.

Choose what you want to earn

Choose what you want to earn

The truth is, it is no harder to earn £1000 per hour, than it is to earn £100 but the activities you need to do to achieve it and probably the people you need to target will be different. But it is a choice. Most businesses don't get this and they end up working for anyone regardless of whether they are a good customer or not.

Most people define their lifestyle by what is left at the end of the month, whereas the really successful people choose a life style and put things in place to pay for it.

Try this as a starting point – it's a very simple calculation but it will help you to get some focus!

So firstly write down what you want to earn in the next 12 months. Not what you need to earn, what you want to earn. So add up all the things you have to pay for, wages, bills, mortgages etc and then add in what you want on top of that, holidays, cars, hobbies etc and come up with a figure.

Then take that number and divide it by how many hours a year you want to work

So if you want to work 7 hours a day with 5 weeks off a year for holidays that gives you 1645 hours of work a year.

That give you a base hour number BUT and it is a big but, none of us can be productive all the time so you need to multiply that number by 3 if you are really productive or more if you are not... (ie you are only doing money earning work 1 in every 3 hours)

Now you have a figure (albeit a basic one) that your time needs to be worth an hour to make the money you want to make.

Do it now...

This year I want to earn _____

Divide that number by the amount of
hours you want to work _____
(235 days x 7hours = 1645)

Multiply that by how productive you can be _____
(for most of us this will be 3 or 4)

What my time needs to be worth an hour _____

How close are you? Is your current model and your current set
of prospects getting you closer to where you want to be – or
further away?

Book bonus available here:
www.marketingjumpleads.com/game-changer-book-bonuses

Be the expert in your market

Be the expert in your market

There are a lot of people doing what you do.

As a global market place there are more people talking than there are listening – so if you want to make your business stand out you need to give people a genuinely compelling reason to talk to you and not the 1000's of other options they can find at their finger tips. Being the expert in your field is a brilliant way of grabbing your slice of the money.

So how do you do it....?   He who talks wins.

If you are waiting for someone else to anoint you as the expert, chances are you are going to be waiting a long time. So it is up to you claim your space as the expert in your field.

A great strategy here is to get stuff written, being the person who "wrote the book on it" will give you a lot of credibility and in an age where there are so many people talking and trust is diminishing, set you apart from the crowd

Things like-

Local press articles, a book, "how to" guides, newsletters, special reports, ebooks, almost anything that people can see you have written will help to cement your position as the person in your industry that everyone turns to for the knowledge.

It's not difficult to do, but like everything in business it needs to be done. Most people will talk a great game but never deliver it into something "physical" – which give you an opportunity. And you don't need to be a national celebrity or bestselling author either.

Whatever you do, whether you are a financial advisor who published the *"7 secrets to financial freedom"* or you sell buttons and write a guide *"on creating classic cardigans"* getting something written down is a really powerful tool.

Think about it, if you are looking for a personal trainer you run a search on Google find 2 possible candidates. One of them is "just another trainer" but the other one has written a book called, "How to Lose Thirty Pounds in 30 Days?"

Which trainer are you more likely to go with?

It's a fact, people give greater reverence to individuals who are published authors. So if you want to more customers, start to appear as the expert in your field then getting stuff written down is one of most important things you can do to make this happen.

Book bonus available here:
www.marketingjumpleads.com/game-changer-book-bonuses

Game Changer Seven

Just do one thing

J.D.O.T. (just do one thing)

Thinking is really important but on its own it isn't going to get you anywhere. You are going to actually have to do something.

And we hope this sounds earth shatteringly obvious, (and it is) but we are constantly astounded by the amount of business owners who are consistently doing nothing to grow their business.

Sound daft? Ask yourself this, have you ever gone a day without some marketing going on in your business? A week? A month? (and NO having a website and going networking does NOT count.)

Most business owners are making no regular effort to bring in new business. And yet they are frustrated that their business doesn't grow.

So why is it?

Well it's normally a combination of time, confidence, fear and being "paralysed" by the ever increasing myriad of marketing options available.

It is true there are a huge amount of options out there and unquestionably you should be trying more of them – but you can't start there. You will become bogged down with overwhelm.

So you need to start with one. Just focus on **one** thing at a time and don't worry about all the other stuff.

What if you just keep it simple and put an hour aside tomorrow just to plan a way to collect some data – maybe put something on your website that was interesting enough for people to leave their details?

What if the next day you wrote a nice follow up email for those that did leave their details?

What if the next day you wrote another email to go and to send them something of interest through the post...?

And whilst we are asking ourselves questions think about this...

What is the worst that could happen? – Someone who wasn't working with you continues not to work with you? That's about as bad as it will get. But at least they now know that you exist!

The BIG difference between the guys that talk a great game and the guys that make the money is **activity**. What they do isn't always perfect and it isn't always successful but they have something CONSTANTLY happening in their business to bring in new clients.

Book bonus available here:
www.marketingjumpleads.com/game-changer-book-bonuses

Dave Carruthers *Voxpopme*

Dave Carruthers
Founder & CEO
Dave has been involved in technology
businesses for the last ten years, and has
been behind a number of successful
startups. His experience as an entrepreneur
and passion for technology drives
Voxpopme's disruptive, innovative approach.

http://voxpopme.com

Paul: So lets dive in, what is it really about for you? Why are you doing this, not necessarily VoxPopMe, but why are you running your own business as opposed to working for someone else?

Dave: Yeah, great question. I guess, from a fairly early age, I kind of always wanted to be responsible for my own destiny and just be in control of where things were going. I mean, the simple answer is, I'm terrible with authority and being told what to do. I think I set my first business up off the back of an experience when I was working for someone building websites and things like that. I think I was ten minutes back from lunch, despite having worked plenty of extra hours and stuff like that, and someone asked me where the hell I'd been and, at that point, I was just like, "I can't work for someone like this. I need to do my own thing." I'm now very conscious of, having started my own business, that I won't be like that with my team. You can't expect people to do the hours, stay late, come in early, and then start lambasting people because they take ten minutes longer on their lunch. It was really just to -- yeah -- just to kind of control my own destiny really.

Paul: Nice. Yeah. It is an interesting one, looking at how other people run their stuff and how you wouldn't want to do it for yourself. So what does success look like for you? What are the physical manifestations or the things -- when you shut your eyes at night, you kind of sleep happy knowing that you have done what you set out to achieve? What does that look like for you?

Dave: I think in the early days, it was very much success was a matter of money, assets, things. Having kind of been relatively successful at a fairly young stage with the work of "The Best Of," and made quite a lot of money, and then lost it all pretty soon after that, going back to zero.

Kind of second time around, I guess, success has been much more defined by lifestyle, experiences, just things like that, less tangible stuff. Yes, it's absolutely focused on growing and scaling the business to size and, ultimately, ambition is to grow it and exit it in some shape, I would say. But I think a realisation, actually, it's about the journey more than the destination.

Paul: That's really interesting. I think it's something that a lot of business owners who have been around, even for kind of a couple of years, are starting to notice and move towards. It needs to be more about that. You've got to enjoy it. Doing what we do, you have to enjoy the journey. I think, if you only aim for an endpoint, it becomes enormously frustrating.

Dave: Well, there is no endpoint because if they say, "What's your endpoint?" Is it I drive a Ferrari? Is it I've got a yacht? Is it any of these things? Whatever endpoint you get to, you'll still pull your yacht into whatever port you're in, and then they'll be someone with a much bigger one. Wherever you end up, from that perspective, it's still a constant battle with things so you have to look at things outside just material gain.

Paul: As you said you been there, done it, lost it and are back bigger than before. Why do you think you've done so well?

Dave: Hustle, I would say. You've got to get up and go, you've got to talk to people. You need to dream big, that was one of the things that I did probably pick up from previous work life. You need to kind of believe what you can do can be as big as it can be.

A great example of that is what we are doing now. It would have been very easy for us to start a company, focus on the UK. Even some of our advisors were, like, we shouldn't launch internationally until we hit £50,000 a month in revenue or we're at break even and stuff. My approach was the world has changed, and, obviously, this isn't applicable for all businesses, but certainly if you're in any kind of technology business, it has to be global. So, within 17 months of us launching, we had offices in Singapore, people in the US, and became a truly global business at a very early stage.

Paul: On the other side of that, then, and I know you'll have seen it with some of the other stuff you've done, why do you think most business owners, or certainly a large amount of them, they struggle and, ultimately, fail?

Dave: I think my approach to growing a business has been to find the right people, surround myself with good people, both within the team that work within the business and then, also, from an advisory perspective.

And, also, some people obviously they cling onto equity. They're very much, this is my business, and I need to have all the equity, or I need to be the owner, whereas we couldn't have achieved what we've achieved without raising investment. We've raised about two and a half, three million pounds over the first three years from various angel investors within that community. We've done that very carefully. A lot of companies, they raise too much money, and they put away too much pressure on themselves and then they can't deliver what they've said. We've raised it almost in a little-and-often fashion, hitting our milestones, getting a group of investors that believe in where we're going as a company. They understand that technology companies that are scaling do require more capital than they're going to generate. So I think that's really helped us.

Paul: I think the capital thing is really important. We see a lot of business owners that really do struggle because they simply don't have the money. They could get it, but they're clinging onto everything and clinging onto that "we mustn't borrow, we mustn't spend", and as such, where they need to get to is just blocked by this massive hurdle, and they can't actually move through it.

Dave: Yeah. I mean, you can't grow a business if you're working hand-to-mouth because you're doing everything, driving it. What's going to happen in a month's time? How am I going to pay...

Paul: Trying to run a business hand-to-mouth is tough not least because that kind of pressure cuts into your "creative headspace" but if you are serious about growing it's all but impossible.

Dave: Yeah. There are different types of businesses, some that require capital, others that can grow organically out of capital generated. But, certainly, in the space that I've been in, in technology, the investment is very much you invest up front in the technology, into the platform, into the software, into resource.

Once you've built it, you've then got to go out and sell it, and what we've been doing is something new to the market, so you've then got to educate the market. And my experience is everything takes longer than you anticipate. Even when you're cautious with your projections and things like that, dealing with our clients that are Fortune 500 companies, the likes of Google and EBay and Tesco and people like that, everything takes a lot longer than you want. Even when you've got a great product, even when people are excited about it, the fact is everything takes longer. So you've just got to allow for that. You can't afford to run out of money just because things are taking longer.

Paul: Looking back, is there one particular thing that stands out that you wish you could go and tell first business Dave about? Is there one thing that you'd wish you'd known when you'd started?

Dave: I think definitely. I think there's a few things, looking back. It's been a succession of mistakes, but every mistake has been a great learning opportunity. Certainly, I think the makeup of the team is one of the biggest, most critical parts. You have to get people that fit your organisation culturally. I think this whole kind of hire slow, fire fast couldn't be more true. We've had people where they weren't right, and we let it go on too long which is definitely one of the things that, in hindsight, I wish we hadn't done.

And then another thing is you have to have conviction and trust your gut feel. It's great to have advisors. It's great to have other input and stuff, but, ultimately, you're running the business. Even when you've got external investors, you're running the business, and you have to back yourself.

Paul: If you could do it all over again, is there one thing that you'd be like "Yeah, I'd tell myself to go and do this better, " or "I'd tell myself to go do this sooner," or something like that?

Dave: Yeah. I think it comes to at the formation stage of a company. So if you're not a sole operator, you're setting up a company, and you've got different people putting in different levels of effort and things like that. Just making sure that that initial equity split is rational and fair because it happens a lot. People split companies equally, or they do this, and people don't always commit. Trying to resolve that further down the line is tough. It's very easy to solve when the company's worth 10 quid and everyone's putting a pound in. Two years down the line, when it's worth five million, it's a bit more difficult. So it's just things like reverse vesting would be a better way to do things rather than just giving away the equity at the start.

Paul: You talk about a bit of your growth there. Has there been a particular strategy or particular thing that you can point towards that has been most instrumental in taking this business from kind of the balance sheet is zero to wherever it is today?

Dave: Yeah. I think social proof has been huge. Success makes success. So once we managed to get a handful of flagship clients, there's almost self-validation. When you can say, oh, so-and-so at company X, Y and Z already use this, it's huge. So, obviously, in the first instance, we did a lot of cold outreach. We used LinkedIn quite a lot to get into the right people.

Persistence has been huge. Our salespeople that are most successful are the people that don't send three emails, don't hear back, and then just think, okay, they're not interested. It's the person who sends email eight, email nine, email ten. Direct marketing has worked very well for us. We've done these video brochures that we send through the post. You think as a video-based tech company, we wouldn't be doing direct marketing, but that's been what's really worked. The clients say, "I get so many emails, I get so many download pages, webinars, eBooks, all this stuff. It was interesting to get something that was interruptive through the post." That's been a kind of great strategy, great strategy for us.

Paul: If you were going to give a bit of advice to a business owner, this is someone you know is going to make it, but they're in that rabbit in the headlights, driving in the dark kind of time. What would be the biggest bit of advice you could give them?

Dave: I guess there are two things that business owners need to be successful staying power and hustle. You just have to keep at it, you have to be relentless. I'm reading a great book at the moment. It's called 10X. The people that are successful, they make 10 times the calls, they do 10 times the followup, they do 10 times the effort, and stuff. It really is, if you put the effort in and are persistent and have hustle, and don't take no for an answer, you will get there. It's just about having perseverance.

Paul: That was really useful, buddy. Massively, massively appreciate your time on that. Thank you very much. It has been massively inspiring to watch you. I still very much remember you heading out for lunch and buying a Porsche and me heading out for lunch and buying a ham and cheese sandwich. I remember thinking, I need to aim a little bit bigger here...

Don't waste time on social media

Don't waste time on social media
- with bonus of full Social Media Mastery Course

Social media is now completely embedded in our lives. The marketing landscape has changed forever and every business owner, big or small, has a huge opportunity.

It's easy though to get carried away and mistake lots of posts and shares with genuine business benefits – revenue and profits. Most UK business owners are only skimming the surface and sadly leaving opportunities and profits untapped and wasting lots of time.

There are 4 key parts of a proper social media strategy. Most of us only tick one or two boxes on this checklist of four, but you need to be embracing all of them to warrant the time and energy and enjoy the success and return on investment all the effort deserves.

Here's a brief run-down on all four steps and their key objectives, then we'll get into the detail on how to actually do it.

SOCIAL LISTENING – Monitoring and responding to customer service and reputation management issues on the social web.

Helps you: Manage reputation - Increase retention - Reduce refunds - Identify product gaps .

SOCIAL INFLUENCING - Establishing authority in the social world, often through the distribution and sharing of valuable content.

Helps you: Increase engagement - Increase website traffic – lets prospects know about your offers - Grow retargeting lists (See Game Changer Second bite of the cherry)

SOCIAL NETWORKING – Finding and associating with authoritative and influential individuals and brands in the social world.

Helps you: "Earn" media mentions - Develop strategic partnerships. PR on-line if you like.

SOCIAL SELLING – Generating leads and sales from existing customers and prospects

Helps you: Generate Leads - Grow Email List - Cross Sell & Upsell - Increase buyer frequency.

SOCIAL MEDIA GOALS

Just like anything in life, you need to have a route map. Most business owners don't often bother with a clear plan when it comes to social media. They rush in, post a few updates and expect the sales to come flooding in. The cardinal sin is to JUST do Social Selling. That's like going to a party and talking about yourself all night. No one will be interested and will actively avoid you.

So you need a plan and you need to measure if that plan has worked.

Book Bonus available here:
It's so important we're going to give you a full
Social Media Mastery Course
www.marketingjumpleads.com/game-changer-book-bonuses

This course includes how to plan the four key steps to social media success, what tools you'll need and how you'll measure your social voice.

Once you have a plan it's easy to pick the right social platforms to concentrate on. As we always say it's better to do one or two really well than skim lots and succeed at none.

"80% Of Success Is Just Showing Up"

Woody Allen

So true.

If all four steps seem daunting at first, master the consistency of posting good quality content to start building your following and trust of your perfect clients. DAILY. Consistency is the key. You can later add-in the social selling funnels, as by then you'll have an engaged and interested audience.

So show-up. Be human. Be authentic. Don't be scared to network.

People will then move naturally through from being AWARE of your business, EVALUATE your skills or products and some will go to BUY.

Making sales and increasing profits is after all the end game from all this work.

Become a welcome guest not an annoying pest

Become a welcome guest not an annoying pest

With all the marketing messages out there people don't want you annoying them. Battering them over the head with your sales pitch.

How annoying are those phone calls about PPI potential claims or the cold callers at your front door? Most of us find these interruptions to our day pests at best.

Yet many business owners drive their marketing on this basis. Bullishly bashing his or her sales message down the throat of anyone who will listen.

When we help business owners with their marketing it is our job to ensure they are 'welcome guests' not 'annoying pests' and that involves getting three things right: -

Firstly what is your **message?** What do you want to say to past, present and future prospects that is compelling, that is magnetic, that cannot be ignored, that must be responded to, that draws people to you like moths to a light? Do you have a great 'message'?

Secondly **who** are you saying it to? Are you taking a scattergun, annoying pest approach and shouting at everyone, or clearly, efficiently magnetising your target audience.

Thirdly, **how** are your delivering that appealing message? What media are you using to attract people towards your light? Different stimulus for different people is needed. The more you know your audience the easier it will be to be welcome in their world.

If you want to increase your conversion rates, close more sales, attract more customers become their 'friend'. We all welcome with open arms friends into our your office, our home, our life.

Yet we are all weary of strangers especially ones who just keep trying to sell to us!

So find the right time of day to approach your audience, offer help, give away advice...you must be the equivalent as the guest for dinner who brings wine and compliments the cooking. You will be invited back.

Book bonus available here:
www.marketingjumpleads.com/game-changer-book-bonuses

Outspend your competition

Outspend your competition

Most business owners automatically take the wrong decision to spend as little as they can get away with to attract and keep their clients. This is simply nuts!

Everyone in your market place is asking what is the cheapest thing they can do get more business. So do it differently (as always) and work out how much you can afford to pay. Spend the most you can and we promise the quality of your leads will explode and your marketing will become easy.

You will be fishing in empty waters and new customers will be easy to catch and keep.

This will be a mind shift for most of you...but a very important one to make. Outspend every marketer in your niche and the rewards will be rich.

By outspending your competitors you can buy speed and growth and leave them feeling discouraged. For this to work you need to know your numbers. What is your new client worth to you? We don't mean what is the average first sale price...we mean what will they spend, on average, over the next twelve months or even what is their lifetime value?

One you have this number it will become obvious what you can spend to attract a new client. It may even be wise to make a loss on their first sale. If you have the willingness to invest properly in acquiring new clients and you have a good on-going strategy to maximise their value, you give yourself a huge commercial advantage. You may even be able to afford media that others can't. TV?

By outspending you can also give extra value to a customer,

which in turn attracts more valuable customers, which gives you more money to spend per customer. Send a DVD player with your DVD preloaded to someone you really want to impress; buy tickets to a concert or big sporting occasion to secure the connection; pick up your dental patients in a limousine.

Show up like no one else can – spend the most you possibly can to get a new customer and you'll attract more valuable customers, which in turn means you reduce the number of overall units you need to sell to reach your target income.

Book bonus available here:
www.marketingjumpleads.com/game-changer-book-bonuses

Dee Woodward *GetitbyDeesign*

Dee is a brand designer, visual linguist, marketing enthusiast and founder of ByDeesign Ltd & Get It.

www.getitbydeesign.co.uk

Paul: So lets start here then. What's it really about for you? Why are you doing what you do as opposed to having a job?

Dee: Honestly, probably because I just got so frustrated working for other people. I've been in business myself six years. So going back six years ago, when I was in my mid-20s, and thought that I knew everything better than everyone that I worked for, and I could do everything better, and that I was going to prove them wrong. They thought I couldn't do anything better than them, and so I decided to jack in my well-paid job and show my boss that I could run a business better than he could.

Paul: Was it just a frustration with the way they were doing it, or what you were actually doing? Is it, "I can't do what I think is best for the client by working for someone else?"

Dee: Yeah. It's very much that. I worked my way through different design agencies, and I was working at a design agency that was doing a lot of signs kind of branding work. I was working with BT and O2 and British Gas, They were all big corporates that you have to jump through a lot of hoops, and getting anything done was so difficult because it was a nightmare to try and actually talk to the person that's really making decisions. There's so many people to go through.

As part of the other side of the agency, we did have smaller businesses, but because they were so used to working in these larger corporations, the way we treated smaller business owners was quite similar. So there would be me working on design for this customer, but I never spoke to the customer. I had to speak to a relationship manager within our company, who then spoke to somebody in their company, who spoke to someone at -- and it was just really frustrating.

All of these people were getting paid well, and I just kept thinking, "Wow, we're charging these small business owners a lot of money to just speak to a lot of different people and not, actually, get anything done." I didn't like it. It didn't work for me. I wanted to be there talking to the business owners and helping them directly.

Paul: With that in mind, what does success look like now? I don't think guys like us ever 'make it', if that makes sense, because there's always a new challenge . But at what point can you kind of look around at your world, at your life, and think, "This experiment has worked,"

Dee: Well, I try to remind regularly myself of what my definition of success is. I've actually achieved it a while ago because for me being successful was having a business that supported the lifestyle that I wanted to have. That meant being able to wake up every day excited about what I was doing for the day, no matter what that was. I mean, I'm not saying that I just sort of run and get into it, jump about and do whatever I want all day. But, most of the time, I do because at the moment what I want to do all day is work with people that I love working with. I've been doing that for the last few years. I will wake up -- if I wake up at 4 a.m., and I'm too excited about a project, I get up and I work on it. That's my choice, and I love it -- so that's kind of my definition of success. That will, obviously, kind of be changing slightly now that I'm a mum. But, hopefully, I've built my business to allow me to kind of step back a bit. For me, I'm kind of living my success every day.

Paul: It's so nice to hear. I think so many people end up living someone else's business dream. I think the vision of success, what it looks to me won't be the same as what it looks like to you, although for us it is actually quite similar. But I think it's really easy for people to end up with their business, doing something that they actually don't really want to do.

Dee: I nearly ended up that way at the beginning because I fell very easily into trying to develop an agency in my business. Actually, there was a lot of reasons why I left that agency environment because I didn't enjoy it, and I didn't want to do that. But, because that's the only way I knew being a designer really, particularly, worked, that's where I kind of saw myself falling into.

So I did manage to snap myself out of that, luckily, before it got too far into kind of employing people and doing a big agency thing. But that was, exactly it, trying to just emulate other people's idea of what success was. Then still, when you read all these big stories about what people are doing all the time, you think, "Oh, that must be what success is." But, actually, sometimes you just have to think about it for yourself and realise that if you don't want a million in the bank or all of these big things, and flashy holidays all the time, and you're quite happy, actually, with your life being enjoyable for you and doing what you love every day, then that's a pretty good place to be.

Paul: I think it's actually quite a brave call to make. I think lots of people, particularly a lot of the guys that we know, we've hung around with, that sort of thing, I think it is quite a big call to make out loud in public, actually, I'm actually happy with 'less'. I don't want all the stuff. It's experiences rather than stuff.

Obviously I know a bit about your business - why do you think you are doing so well?

Dee: Probably because I'm quite stubborn when I've got an idea, and I want to do things my way, and I don't like being wrong. So I've got quite a bit of grit and determination to make things work. I think you do have to have quite a thick skin when you're running a business yourself, and especially I felt being in the creative industry, there's always a lot of stigma around it not being a real kind of job because you're just creating pretty pictures and things. That was a stigma that I had to get over quite quickly because it was really myself that was projecting that, I suppose, a little bit more than, perhaps, other people interpreting it that way.

But, yes, you do kind of grow a bit of a thick skin when you're out there on your own doing it, and you just got to kind of get on with things really. My mantra is to crack the f**k on, and I usually just try and live most days by it. I think that's really got me to where I am at the moment.

Paul: So leading on from that then, why do you think most business owners struggle or fail?

Dee: Probably a mix of listening too much to other people's opinions. It's good to surround yourself with people who you know have a similar mindset to you. I, definitely, get the value in that, but there's also times when you really do need to trust your own judgment and listen to yourself a little bit more than trying to listen to what other people are up to.

So sometimes I think people get swept up too much in what other people's opinions of what they should be doing are, and they lose track of why they went into business in the first place and what's going to make them happy. Then you just end up down this kind of downward spiral where you are doing stuff you don't want to do to get somewhere you don't really want to be. So I think, yeah, I think that's probably one of the biggest things I've seen, people listening to the wrong people and not listening to themselves.

Paul: Let me follow up with that. Is there something that you know now or something that, I don't know, you kind of do as normal now that you wish you'd known or wish you'd done right at day one all those years ago?

Dee: Yes. Not invest so much money in other people's opinions of my business. I wasted a lot of time trying to do things a different way to what I, naturally, thought I should be doing it. It's a tricky one because if I'd not done that, then maybe I wouldn't have got the answers that I needed to for myself.

Paul: It's an interesting one to flag up, because I think a lot of these things you only know it now because of what you've been through, and you wouldn't know it if you hadn't been there But I think, one of the reasons that we're putting this together is that because there will be people out there that are thinking, "You know, I've heard about ABC. Should I be doing it too?" There will be people that are in that battle with themselves almost, "I feel this is right. You're telling me that is right. What do I do?"

Dee: That's a good distinction there, actually. It's knowing, trusting what you believe to be right. So if you feel like there's a particular group or support or mastermind group, for things that you should be a part of because you think it's right, then go for it.

But don't try to get caught up in thinking, "Well, someone's told me that if I'm not willing to invest ten grand a month in this high-flying mastermind, that I'm not going to be a successful business owner." It sounds silly when you say it like that, but we do sometimes get swept up in this mindset of believing that you have to do this. But just trusting that, actually, and finding the right people that support you for what you want to do in your business rather than trying to change it.

Paul: I agree completely, but I also think its really hard to find the right people. Most business owner we meet talk a great game but aren't willing to do anything about it. Most networking rooms are full of people wearing the fact that they haven't had a holiday in 6 months as badge of honor – but yet never do anything about it. And it's those people who are easy to find. Finding the people that will really 'get it' and will actually make the changes and take the action are few and far between.

So if you could do it all over again, what would you do differently? I mean, obviously, you've said you wish you'd known not to invest so much in other people's, but leading on from that, what would you have done differently?

Dee: I think I would have really trusted myself more and got into the online world a lot quicker because I put it off for a while, and there was some stumbling blocks I had to kind of overcome.

Working that bit out and finding a smaller kind of network of people I really trust and who really support me in my growth over the last kind of six months to a year has been invaluable for me. So it's finding those kind of few key people that can really support you, whoever they are or wherever they are. And trusting your kind of gut when it comes to making decisions in your business.

Paul: We've talked a bit about the support element of it, but has there been a particular action or strategy you have used that has helped get your business from where it was to where it is now?

Dee: Yeah. I suppose, really, it's connecting with people who are doing similar things. So I've found people in the online space that are launching similar type of products and services and membership sites and things to me, and I've really just kind of connected with them. We find that, actually, together we've managed to really launch our things separately, but going through the process together and supporting each other has really helped kind of catapult that side of the business.

Paul: I think it is quite a lonely place, a business owner, at some point. Particularly when you've got a lot of knowledge and you read a lot of stuff, you can almost feel paralysed by all the things you could do and . Without having someone close by that you can trust, bounce the ideas off of, just go through stuff with, it can be really difficult.

Dee: It is, definitely. I went through quite a closed period in my business of a year after I had an accident, and I went into being a bit of a hermit for a while because I was recovering. That was probably one of the kind of darker times in my business because I was so cut off from people. So it took me a while to kind of get back out there. When you are doing your business yourself, and you're hiding behind a computer a lot of the time, it's difficult sometimes to get back out and reconnect with people. But that's, definitely, one of the biggest, I think, turning points in my business is reconnecting with people in a face-to-face environment as well, not just online.

Paul: Stop it with your face-to-face now.

Dee: It's crazy.

Paul: You old-timer... Just being with the right people, but being really choosy about who those people are, and almost trying a few. Go for a few people and see if they are actually bringing benefit or just bringing noise and the opportunity to spend some money.

Dee: Yeah, definitely. It's unfortunate there are a few too many of those around, but you got to kiss a few frogs, I suppose, before.

Paul: Or as I call it, the university years. Maybe we'll take that out of the transcript.... As our parting shot then, what bit of advice would you give to a business owner? This is someone that we know is good, they are going to make it because I think we both know there are guys that talk a great game and probably would have a happier lifestyle if they were, actually, in a job. But to guys that we know are going to make it, but they're in that rabbit in the headlight, driving in the dark kind of territory, what would be your biggest bit of advice to help them kind of see it through and take that step change to the next level?

Dee: I would kind of -- a simple one, really, but suggest to actually crack the f**k on and do it and just -- you might have to edit that as well

Paul: No, no. That stays in. That's definitely staying in.

Dee: I think it would have been -- my husband always takes the micky out of me most days now. There's not a day that goes by without someone saying CTFO. You just need a CTFO day. That's the biggest thing for me is just to kind of crack on. You will fail, and you will screw up quite a few times, but do it, and get over it and keep going.

Sell big ticket items

Sell big ticket items

Whether you look at your overall pricing position or add in one or two high ticket services, products or events start planning to sell big ticket items.

The old adage it's far easier to sell one £1million item than sell a million £1 items is so true. Are you solely concentrating on the lower end sales, when inside your business there is a BIG sale item waiting for you to identify it and then sell to your list ?

For a boost in your cashflow think about 2 - 4 events you could run a year that would both position you in front of your clients, but also let your charge top ticket prices. An additional £10K, £20K £50 or even £100K extra a couple of times a year could transform your business.

What premium version of your service or product could you introduce? Think about the service you offer and what your audience would pay more for. Would they pay more to see you rather than your team member? Would they pay more for 'out-of-office' hours appointments, or for a monthly check-up or monitoring service? Would they like a premium online version of your advice; a coaching program, a Mastermind group?

Could you package your products and services together, rename it and sell as a Platinum product? Would your audience pay for a higher priced, higher margin product?

This strategy goes back to looking for the affluent in your sector and seeing how business can meet their demands.

Give some thought to what your 'big-ticket items' can be. This will allow you to raise prices overall, and make the same amount of money with fewer clients.

There is a Big Ticket Item buried in every business ... you just sometimes have to dig deep.

Make your prospects work

Make it "harder" for your prospects to work with you.

This strategy definitely goes against the "conventional wisdom" but done properly it can be a real game changer for your business.

Most people assume that having prospects jump through hoops will dissuade them from doing business from you. However, what can actually happen is you end up working with the better-qualified clients who will value your product or service more.

Take for example a local IFA and Past Mastermind Member. One of the biggest issues in the financial services market is time spent on gathering information. Multiple forms are sent back and forth consequently the process takes longer which means the payments are also slower to arrive.

However this IFA works very differently. She commits to a high level of service and signs an agreement to guarantee that fact but she also insists her customers do the same.

She is very clear that she can make a real difference to the financial future of the "right" people who genuinely want her help (and don't get me wrong she delivers on this) but her customer needs to be serious about it too.

They have to provide paper work and complete a detailed assessment, (which she charges for) before she agrees to take their financial planning on.

Not only do her clients have to prove a sufficient sum to invest initially they also have to sign an agreement to confirm they will provide the information when it is needed.

And whilst in reality she is unlikely to "call the agreement in" it does position her very strongly. It fixes an issue that slows down her income and it cuts out the time wasters.

Is it likely that some people will be put off by her stance? – Certainly but the chances are that those people were never going to be her ideal target clients and would be predisposed to the problems that caused her to change her model in the first place.

As ever there will be more clients than she needs who are happy to work this way and our gut reaction tells us these people will be drawn towards her because of her stance.

And this is a big point – look to work with people that want to work with you – the way you work. It will mean you spend a lot more time doing what you do best and a lot less selling.

You don't need to get silly with it but you can put hurdles in place to get exactly the kind of customers you want to work with. That's the big bonus of working for your self. You get to choose your customers. Choose wisely.

Book bonus available here:
www.marketingjumpleads.com/game-changer-book-bonuses

Words can make you money

Words can make you money
- bonus of Content Marketing Life Cycle

"Traditional Marketing is telling the world you're a rock star. Content marketing is showing the world that you are one"

Content marketing is THE way to find, build and convert an audience of exactly the right people who need your services and products.

The term **Content Marketing** is banded around as the holy grail of modern digital marketing. How can it make your business money instead of sucking up all your valuable time?

Done well, Content Marketing leads directly to more sales and more prospects.

Done badly, it takes a whole load of your time and is frustrating and costly.

Firstly, we are not JUST talking about blogging here.

Content marketing is every word you ever write or speak that is shared about your business. Your content marketing is at every stage of your communications with strangers, prospects and existing customers - articles, blogs, emails, social updates, videos, sales pages, the list is endless.

DO YOU NEED GOOD CONTENT? Hell yes!

The formula is pretty simple. If you create GREAT CONTENT that inspires, educates or entertains then you'll create an audience of followers.

Creating good content takes some effort. The good news is you no longer have to 'guess' at what your audience wants to read or listen to. With the right thought and research the pieces of content you create will resonate with the right people AND have a long shelf life.

So writing a good content article will effectively become an asset for your business. You can utilise these assets in various ways, for different audiences AND keep using them for months, even years to come. So the work involved today has a long-term benefit for your business.

Many of us have produced 'one-hit wonder' blogs or LinkedIn pulse articles, which usually failed miserably as they weren't part of a proper joined-up plan to help our prospects and customers. They simply didn't lead anywhere.

Someone, somewhere said all business owners should all be writing blogs. You've probably long considered this chore as 'something else' on the already bulging 'to-do' list. You may be throwing them up ad hoc and resenting the lost time and effort.
Good news. This randomness can stop today.

AS ALWAYS with any marketing, start with your avatar – the perfect person you'd like to work with. Spending time really understanding this person and where they are in their thought process will help you make deliberate choices on the content you write.

Someone who doesn't even know you exist, isn't aware of your company or even of the services you offer may well need 'warming up' through a great blog post. Simple good content that helps inform, entertain or educate them. (See we told you, your blog does fit in as part of your content plan!)

But if someone has already decided, for example, they need a new car, they will need a different style of content. Here they will be evaluating between different makes and models and a web page showing your car fuel efficiency against major competitors could be the perfect content piece to write. Sending a ready buyer to a blog just won't cut it, in this instance.

Getting into your customers mind makes your content marketing fly.

What are they thinking right now? Have they chosen the car, engine size and colour and are just looking for the right garage to hand over their cash? Content about the guarantee you offer, the service deals included and a bank of testimonials from your satisfied buyers could just be the right content to share at this point to convert the sale.

Content Marketing Success Tip #1

REALLY Understand Your Avatar. Know your customer and determine where they are in their thinking. If you know this you can choose the right channel to post your content on eg a full demo video, posted on YouTube, of a new vacuum cleaner, for someone ready to buy a new model will be the perfect content piece and channel to share this content.

Content Marketing Success Tip #2

Build content at ALL levels of your customer relationship. Giving value-first content to let people discover your business IS very important.

Just don't stop there.

Create great content all the way through your relationship with customers. From the second they are aware of you through to buying customers, content can cement and continue to excite relationships.

Content Marketing Success Tip #3

Content Should Lead To The Next Step...

Failure to not provide the next logical step in your 'relationship' with your content for consumers is not only bad marketing, it also gives a bad user experience.

If a visitor to your car website has landed on your page, found a car they like and seen your efficiency and testimonial comparison page, they now want to test drive. MAKE IT EASY FOR THEM TO BOOK. The next logical step is to try the vehicle.

So have live booking facilities, or an instant call back option. Let them know what a test drive involves, what they need to bring, create the excitement. Make the next step super easy to take.

If they have to go searching for your number, reach an answer machine or fill out a long sign-up page your 'content' has failed.

Content Marketing Success Tip #4

Ask for the sale. There has been so much made of 'value-first content marketing' that we've forgotten to ask for the sale!

You're a first date with someone (don't ruin it with a marriage proposal!). It's ok though to ask for a second date. In fact, it's a good thing to lead them to the next step as we've already discussed. If you went on a date and didn't ask for another date then you're effectively saying you're not interested.

That's what many business owners are doing right now. They are orchestrating the perfect first date. Writing a super useful blog, getting people to read it.... then doing NOTHING.

Content should impress – intrigue – entertain - educate and even amuse. Just don't forget it needs ultimately to lead to a sale.

Book Bonus available here:

Content Marketing Life Cycle will help you plan the right words for the right customers at the right time.

www.marketingjumpleads.com/game-changer-book-bonuses

Jodie Bidder *Sami Tipi*

Jodie and her husband Craig run Sami Tipi, the UK's most loved Tipi Weddings Supplier and Organiser.

Driven and direct Jodie has taken Sami Tipi from a standing start to a highly sort after business with people booking years in advance just to secure their services.
http://www.samitipi.co.uk/

Paul: So lets start simple – why do you run your own business?

Jodie: For us, it's all about being your own boss, being in charge of your own time, your own destiny. Being able to have time with the family when you want time with the family, to be able to go to on holiday without having to ask anybody. That's huge. Really import-ant. It's just being in charge of your own destiny, really, with the way you're going. You're responsible for what happens, where you live or work, and your own business. Our business creates very much a nice lifestyle for us, and a place where we want to go to when are we are working.

Paul: That's interesting. So many people we've spoken to it is about ensuring their business delivers a lifestyle. On that route then, so what does success look like? How do you know the work you're putting in is worth it? What's happening around you? What does that look like?

Jodie: I think there's definitely a mountain in front of you, and even when you get to the top of where you set it when you're at the bottom, you realise when you get there, actually, there's more of a mountain. You just keep moving your own goals, moving your own goal posts. Something else to strive towards. But then, when you get feedback from the industry professionals, your own customers that appreciate what you do, see what you do, that in itself, that recognition is for me a big measure of success. It shows that you are moving in the right direction. Sometimes it's nice just to stop on that mountain and turn around to see how high you have actually climbed. You need to take stock.

Paul: It is vital to stop sometimes and look at what you have done, how far you have come. Most business owners never do this, and often they just wrap themselves up in the stress of the next thing. I think you have to enjoy the journey. Doing what we do, you have to enjoy the journey. And it's a stupid thing to say, but you have to enjoy the bad times as much as the good. I think if you are waiting for this perfect "situation" you are just going to look back in years to come and realised you missed so much good stuff. Your business is ONLY there to deliver a lifestyle and particularly as a small business owner that means you need to enjoy the journey... even when it is a bit rubbish.

Jodie: Yeah, absolutely. It is holding onto that. We all have rubbish days, and we can sometimes go, "Aw, I'm sure it would be easier if I was employed again, doing this for someone else" But, no, you have rubbish days when you're employed. So it's taking stock, so, actually, one bad day in the grand scheme of things is fine. That's all part of the journey. Life is better doing it as a business owner on your own journey than doing it for somebody else. Because it doesn't matter what you do, you're always going to have bad days, but those good days far outweigh those bad days.

Paul: Yeah. I think if someone asked the question of me, it's freedom of choice, to be able to do what I want, when I want to do it, if I want to do it. I know I could work more and earn more, but I choose to have time with the family, time with the kids. I love the fact that, if need be today, I can just disappear for a week or two. Potentially, the business won't move forward as fast, but it probably -- because of the way I've set it up, it's not going to retreat. You never know, but it is -- that's been a big measure for us.

Jodie: That's right.

Paul: That really is success when. I can, literally, choose it all. So looking at all of the stuff you've done, you guys are smashing it. Why do you think you guys have done so well?

Jodie: [Laughing]. Oh, dear. Don't put the laughter in.

Paul: No, no. It's all going in. I don't know how you transcribe laughter.....

Jodie: Let's see. I think it's that determination and that vision of where you want to go. We're a husband and wife team, and we also know each other's strengths and each other's weaknesses too. But, as a client the feedback that we get is that they buy into us and as a couple who both do what they do best to look after them.

I think it is the personal service that we offer everybody. I heard a couple say to us, "I felt like I was the only client, the only couple, the only wedding that you were dealing with, and I hadn't realised until I was told how many events you've got this year, that you've got that many. I really felt like we were the only customer that you'd got." That, for us, again, is a big kick that we're moving in the right direction, we're doing a great job. We're moving where we want to go, succeeding. That is just testament, in itself, that one sentence.

Paul: That's lovely. Again, I think, not wanting to put words in your mouth, but it's almost of the it's the importance of "how over what".

Jodie: Yeah, absolutely. It has to be all about the customer experience, the customer journey, and helping them through a process, guiding them through a process. Not making decisions for them, but giving them the right information to help them make decisions, and just taking them through that journey. Having an experience with it as well. A pleasant experience, of course.

Paul: We may have answered it, but looking at the other side of it then, why do you think most business owners struggle or fail?

Jodie: Sometimes I think it's fear of not going for it. I can remember when we first about to go on this journey, and I remember sitting on my floor at home rocking, saying, "Craig, are we doing the right thing? Is this right for us?" Craig said, "Jodie, we've come this far. Yes, it is." It was the case that we were ready to hit go on the website, hit live. I remember saying to Craig, "speak to your dad. What does he say?" Now, he's employed. Of course, he said, "Get a job." I said, "Forget that. Let's do it. We know we're doing the right thing."

It was taking yourself completely out of that comfort zone, and I think you have to do that regularly. Take yourself out of your comfort zone. It's the only way we're going to grow because if you don't, you become stagnant, you don't move forward. You've got to look at fear in the eye, move forward with it. Take yourself out of your comfort zone. That's when great things happen.

We've launched a book ourselves. We got great results from that. But people that just become stagnant don't move forward, don't invest in themselves. Then invest time to learn, to move forward, to keep up with trends, technology, and everything else. Don't become stagnant. Just keep moving forward.

Paul: Looking back to those kind of days now since you sat rocking, is there something that you know now that you'd wish you'd known when you started?

Jodie: I think it was that assurance that it will be okay. It will all work out. It might not be the path that you thought you'd take, but it was always the path you were supposed to take. It'll get you there.

Paul: I think it's so easy to get yourself paralyzed by fear, paralyzed by the enormity of it, and you just don't make that first step. I think it's like going for a run when you really don't want to go for a run. The hardest step is the first one out the door because once you're there, you're off and you go, and you've taken the hardest step. But it's so easy just to sit and plan, we see it a huge amount with businesses that put all their time, energy, effort and money, into creating this beautiful thing – whether it's a product or service. But they never put any energy effort and money into how they are actually going to get a customer. The planning is the easy bit. the product, the offering. Getting your first customer. That's the hardest bit. And that is the bit they never think about how that's going to happen. They are forever getting ready, is that kind of paralysis by fear and what happens if they don't do it and no one buys it. You've got to get that first step out the door. Once you're across the doormat, your next step is so much easier.

With that assurance in mind then, if you could do it all over again, or you were to do it, what would you do differently?

Jodie: I don't think that we would. The timing was all right for us. When we first started out, we assessed our own skills to make sure that we were balanced in the setup, which actually meant Craig keeping on a full-time job. I was full-time in the business. We got our business up and running so we'd still got some financial income to pay the bills. And then at a point, he left and was full-time in this business, which, actually, came a whole 12 months sooner than we'd anticipated or planned for. But our whole business has always been a year ahead of where we've always planned for. It moved quicker than what we ever anticipated. Would I change anything? No, I wouldn't.

Paul: From a point of view of getting from where you were when you started to where you are now, has there been a particular strategy, a particular thing that you've done that you'd point to as that has been the most powerful thing, the most potent thing we've done?

Jodie: I think forward it's all been about building relationships, building relationships with our industry suppliers, building relationships with our landowners, building relationships with our customers, and our staff as well. I think that's what it's all been about because then those people that we've built relationships with talk about us. That social proof where other people are talking about us is stronger than anything I can throw money at.

Paul: That's really interesting. I think lots of people see it as a nice thing, having good relationships is lovely. But they're not seeing it as much of a physical marketing strategy as running some Facebook ads or doing email marketing. I think it is something that is missed by a lot of businesses.

Jodie: It's getting out there. In the early days when you're set up from the kitchen table, there's no denying those times were actually lonely. You sat on your own at your kitchen table. Most people communicate these days via email. They don't have a physical conversation. You could go a couple days without having a physical conversation within your work environment. It's not denying that those early days were lonely. That's why, again, it's important to get out there and go on workshops, train, meet other people, talk to other people that's in a similar situation, and don't lose focus in those early days of where you're going because, as I say, those early days can be a lonely time.

Paul: Yeah, I think so. I think that is so important to hang around with some people in those early days.

Jodie: With like-minded people. Yeah, absolutely.

Paul: Dig out those right people and just kind of follow it and just be there. Spend some time. Force yourself into a room with them.

As our finishing maneuver then, if a business that came to you for help, What would be your biggest bit of advice to them?

Jodie: What we just said, go out, hang around with the right people. Invest time in yourself. Dedicate real time to, see it as an important part of the business. Have a default diary so that one day a week or a month you dedicate time investing in yourself, learning, networking, talking to like-minded business people. Surround yourself with the right people that when you're having a bad day, you know you can pick the phone up to them, and they pull you back up to where you need to be so you can move straight on quickly. Really important. Don't stay in a low. Just change something to move forward quickly.

Yeah. Surround yourself with the right people, take time out to invest in yourself because that's what helps your business grow. That's why joining Marketing Jumpleads was so useful,

I found the right people to mix with, spend time with. But, also, I found people I needed to help me things like to redesign my website, help me with branding. It's a great place to network.

But JumpLeads itself, as well, it also joined the dots. A great example of this is we had a web page from a particular website. We used Instagram. What JumpLeads taught me was to have a dedicated page for Instagram. It just joined the dots. So now, when someone goes on Instagram, that page links back to a dedicated Instagram page on our website, which has information that they need. It was just joining those dots.

Put your prices up

Put your prices up

As strategies go this is the simplest one out there, but experience shows that making a price increases is often the one that business owners struggle with the most.

It's simple in the fact that it is just a number. It's a quick change of a web page or a different number in your next customer conversation and that's it - your prices are up, it actually is that simple.

So why do so many businesses find it so difficult, well it often come down to two key points

   1)   They think they will stop getting new business
   2)   They think existing customers will leave

The truth is however for many customers, (and especially existing customers) price is NOT the deciding factor. People buy at a price they think is valuable and the reality is that in the majority of cases the business owner is more hung up on the prices than their customers are.

Take for an example a local voice coach and Marketing Jumpleads member. Voice coaching is traditionally a fairly low priced sale with £20 – £30 per hour being fairly standard for the industry and this was exactly where he was charging a year and a half ago - as were all his competitors.

Fast forward 18 months and he has gone from charging £20 per hour to £85 per hour (that's an increase of 425%!!). He has more customers than he has ever had,. He works far less hours and it has also had the desired affect of reducing (to almost zero) the 'time wasters". His product is EXACTLY the same but he is just charging more for it.

It's not all about big numbers. If you charge £15 per hour and you put it up to £17– how many customers would you lose over £2 per hour – almost certainly none – but you have just increased your PROFIT by 14%.

And the BIG question: how many customer would you lose if you doubled your prices today. 10%? 20%? 50%? Think about it. If you doubled your prices you could afford to have half as many customers as your currently have.

And who are your 'trouble' customers – the ones that cause you the most grief? Are they the ones who pay you the most or the least?

We see it again and again, business owners put their prices up and nothing happens except higher profits. Their customers see the value in their service and their prospects see the credibility that comes with a higher price.

Don't spend time worrying about it, just try it today and see what happens.

Book bonus available here:
www.marketingjumpleads.com/game-changer-book-bonuses

Say the right thing in the right way

Say the right thing in the right way

A lot of marketing messages are really not 'Messages' at all. They're just 'business cards' - name, rank and serial number. Who we are, what we do, where we are.

We've looked at WHO you are targeting...now let's think about what are you going to say to them. Use the right language and media that is totally appropriate for who you want to impress.

If you are trying to attract restaurant owners talk about 'covers' not clients. If you are getting a message to mums at home what is the best medium, time of day and language to appeal to them?

Often using 'every day' language rather than stuffy corporate jargon can give your messages personality and volume. One tip is to record a voice memo of what you want to say, before you type it up. That way the words are 'real' and often carry a sentiment and passion lost in words typed straight to the keyboard.

Just reciting facts or failing to give a clear call to action is not a strong enough message. Make sure your message clearly sells your unique selling proposition (USP). Tell us what you can do to make us part with our cash. What benefit can you bring to my life. What worry or passion will you satisfy? How will I feel before and after I've booked your service?

What problem, desire or itch can you scratch. If your perfect client asked for your help what would they say? Your message should answer that quest for help. Your message rather than reciting a list of features should speak to your target audience loud and clear so they stop what they are doing and know you are speaking to them.

It will be unlikely that you will get your message right from day one. Trial different messages. Test the results and keep going until one of them resonates with your audience, that becomes your control. Now get that message out there loud and clear to your perfect prospect.

Game Changer Sixteen

Follow-up

Follow-up

Most business owners are leaving a lot of money on the table simply by not following-up. What do we mean? By doing nothing or very little after someone has shown an interest in your business or they've even bought from you.

When was the last time you spent you money with a business and received a thank you? When was the last time you enjoyed a meal in a great restaurant and never heard from them again?

Every aspect of the customer journey through your business gives you an exciting opportunity to add follow-up steps that will give you three advantages over your competitors –

1. You will overcome 'buyers remorse' and help your customers feel delighted they have spent with your business.

2. You create multiple opportunities to upsell and cross sell.

3. You can educate, inspire, wow and remind potential and existing clients that you are THE business they need when the time is right for them to buy.

Start simple and create a few follow-up steps at a time. For example what happens when a new client has asked for a quote or made an on-line enquiry?

Some ideas of follow-up steps to consider:

*   Mail a free report
*   After an immediate email quote, send a written version of the quote with a handwritten note
*   Include a booklet of testimonials
*   Forward a useful DVD, article, or booklet
*   Schedule a follow-up phone call to check reports and quotes have arrived

- Send a letter with a countdown offer
- Postcard reminder of an offer
- Start sending monthly newsletters

Don't leave your prospects and clients floundering. Take control of the image they have of you and the future conversation. If you are sending useful, helpful follow-up steps you will attract clients. FACT. Don't be too polite. KEEP GOING. Research varies but you need to follow-up at least 7 times to turn a cold prospect into a paying client.

Book bonus available here:
www.marketingjumpleads.com/game-changer-book-bonuses

Val Mattinson *Benessamy*

Val Mattinson
Creative Director
Benessamy Weddings & Events

Val started her career as a solicitor in the public sector before moving into external and corporate affairs where she started her journey into event planning, organising corporate, ministerial and special events.

Having trained with the UK Alliance of Wedding Planners (UKAWP), Val launched Benessamy in 2011 and is now a Level 2 Member of the UKAWP and has been appointed as their Regional Ambassador for the Midlands.

Val was awarded the Best Wedding Planner in the East Midlands in The Wedding Industry Awards 2015 and 2016 following client nominations and voting and Highly Commended in the Nationals in 2015.

Val is an active member of the UK wedding industry and provides venue consultancy and business mentoring. She regularly hosts networking events for businesses within the industry.
http://www.benessamy.co.uk/

Paul: So, my first question, what is it really about for you? Why do you do what you do as opposed to having a job, if that makes sense?

Val: I have to say I spent a long time working for all sorts of amazing businesses and organisations. I spent quite a long time in the public sector and enjoyed that. But I think, increasingly, I just found that it was the creativity that I really enjoyed, I wasn't really having the opportunities for it, if that makes sense. Because I think, even working at the level that I did in my last job, where I was in charge of a large department responsible for the strategy and delivering it, but you still worked under the reign of another organisation, of another person's goals, another person's top targets. They weren't mine. It wasn't my vision. I was helping to deliver somebody else's.

I really enjoyed being able to set my own and I try to make it as challenging as possible because I don't like to feel too comfortable at all, not stretched. I like to feel that I'm challenging myself to make that better each time.

I think even at the highest level in another organisation, in another business that isn't yours, you don't have that same freedom, that same opportunity to be creative, and actually do something, and make a difference that is actually from your own kind of things, if you see what I mean.

Paul: Yeah. I absolutely get it. It's a similar sort of thing to me. I love what I did in all of my jobs, really. Laterally, I just felt it go in a direction that was neither right nor wrong, but it just wasn't the direction I wanted it to go in. At that point, you either suck it up and take your chances, or you decide to not and kind of bumble on. There's no right or wrong on this, but, yeah, I get it completely. I just couldn't do what I felt I wanted to do and what I felt I could do the best to help the other folk by doing what I was currently doing.

So what does success look like to you? How do you know when you've got there?

Val: I want to start, I think, by saying I'm not there yet. It is quite interesting because it's all relative. So I mentor business owners. I spent quite a lot of time with other people saying, "Oh, you're really successful. Can you help us do that?" And I sometimes think I'm successful, I'm still constantly looking at others and noting what they're doing. I don't think we ever stop learning, and I don't think we ever reach a point where we say, you know what, I've finished. I really enjoy getting up and doing what I do. The day that it stops feeling like that, and I don't enjoy it as much, is the day I need to stop doing it because if you're only half doing it, then you're in the wrong thing.

In terms of success now, I think if I was looking back, if I was 10 years ahead, I hope that what I'm looking at is something I've created where I've got people working with me in the business, enjoying it as much

I enjoy it, and I'm giving them the opportunity to be as creative as I have been in that business. I don't think that, for me, success is all about the material things. I mean, yes, of course, like many other people, I'd love to say, yes, I drive this or I live here. But, ultimately, for me, it's about, I know it sounds trite, but it is about happiness, and it's about fulfilment. It's definitely about feeling as though it's worthy of spending time. If I wanted something that just earned me lots of money, I could have stayed doing my old job, to be honest. It paid well. It was never about money. I did not leave there because it wasn't paying me enough. It paid well. So I'm not driven by that feeling. My business needs to make money, but it's not really that, it's not what it's all about, I don't think, for me.

Paul: I do agree, my driver has never been the cash but you need it. I have a lovely life, but it is because of the happiness not the money, but I think lots of people miss it. Lots of business owners just forget that, and they get trapped in the more bigger, more bigger, without reevaluating, why? What do I actually need? What really makes me happy?

Val: Yes it's something you said earlier, back to why you started doing what you're doing, in the first place. As your business develops, and as your business grows, there's a need to sort of stop and take stock. So it might be that you have to accept that you can't do everything yourself. You do have to get help in. Because, actually, what I was finding was I was spending probably more hours than when I worked full-time. and my family were complaining that, actually, I was doing too many hours then and not getting enough chance to enjoy my life. It is a balance. I work hard to make my business and work well, but I'm doing it so that I have a good life, as well, and I enjoy time with my family and my friends.

So if it all becomes too one sided and the scales just become so unbalanced that's not success for me It will be when those scales are balanced. I'm running a successful business, and I'm having a great life because of that and not the other way around, if that makes sense.

Paul: Yeah, I know, it absolutely does. I know you said you're not there yet, but you are doing much better than most in your industry and beyond. What do you think has been the difference between you and them, if that makes sense?

Val: I try really hard to make sure that, as much as I look for inspiration and ideas in a range of places, I really try hard to continue with the view, which is I am my competition. I'm my worst enemy. I'm the person who will hold me back from doing the things I want to do. It really isn't about others. And if you have that in your head, I was like that as a child. I was like that as a teenager. I was like that in my first jobs. But the thing that stops me from, say, giving something a go is actually the voices inside, not outside.

So if I think I really want to do that, I've always wanted to go to that place, I try really hard to block out other people saying, "Well, you're never going to do that. That'll never work. That'll never happen." Because, actually, sometimes it's me going, "Oh, my God, I don't know if I can manage that. I'm not sure if I can really enter into that competition, or I'm not sure if they all want to talk to me about this big business idea." And it's almost like trying to ignore that and just constantly keep trying.

And I think sometimes people like to see somebody that is trying really hard. I don't always manage it. Try really hard to be as positive as I can in terms of the outlook for my business or myself, which I think rubs off. Positivity rubs off in the same way that negativity rubs off.

Paul: So on the reverse side to that, though, why do you think most business owners struggle, or, indeed, fail?

Val: I think a number of things. I think there's a mixture of speaking to and hanging out with the wrong people. And I mean that in a way that I was saying about positivity, negativity. Surround yourself with positive, inspiring, interesting people. I think that helps you to be more positive, more inspiring, more interesting. I think you should, in terms of networking is probably a really good example. I think there are times when you should network with people at the similar stage to you as your business, and there are times when it's really good to network with people at more advanced stage in your business. If you spend too much time with one and not the other, it can have a negative effect on your business, and vice versa.

So if you spend lots of time with people who are much more advanced than you in your business, and you're somebody who constantly is looking at them, thinking, "Oh, my God, look at where they are. My business isn't that," as opposed to, "One day I want to be doing something like that, and I've got it in me to do it," that can be positive. As opposed to coming around and thinking, "I'm never going to be like that."

I give you a different example in terms of your house and garden. I used to live next door to neighbours and their house was immaculate. We'd pop over for coffee and whatever, come back and go, "Oh, my God." But they didn't have young children. They didn't have toy boxes and like Teletubby stuff everywhere. It's not comparing like with like. The house was the same house, i.e., it was on an estate, but the houses were very similar. But, actually, their lifestyle was very different. Their children were both grown up. They were living, in fact, very different lives, which I say that to business owners I work with. My children are now in their late teens and at university and about to go off to Uni, and they are self-sufficient now. They still need you to do things, but it's very different to waking up and looking after young children. And I've seen business owners struggling with trying to manage those sorts of home-life challenges and running a business, as well. Trying to live out someone else results but with a different scenario

So you do have to ask for help, I think, along the way. I think that's the case no matter how many years you've been in business. I think the help that you need is just different.

Paul: It comes up again and again, spending time with the right people, I think, it's huge. It is huge. I think lots of people either overlook it or don't actually think about it. They just think, well, people say I should spend time with people – it's the networking example, again - I'm off out networking without thinking, are those people driving you, are they pushing you on?

I remember when I first started, I would go networking, and I didn't enjoy it because the people in the room were really uninspiring, and I remember I drove into the car park one day, and I had the best car, let's not a particularly big car, or most modern or whatever. But I'm not a car guy at all, it has no passion for me, but I just remember thinking, what am I going to learn from these guys? It isn't all about a big car. A big car is not the measure of success for lots of people. But I do remember thinking, I'm just starting out here, and what am I going to get from these guys? That was the day that I stopped just hanging around with any people and looking for the right people, people that were better than me, people that could teach me more.

Val: It's huge, isn't it? I think when you said about why do some business owners fail lots of times. I think you do have to find a safe place, as well, in whichever way, if it's a physical place or a virtual place, but you do need to find a place where you can put your hand up sometimes and say, "I'm struggling with this, " or "I can't make this work." I'm seeing people doing that in the wrong place. It's different for different people. Whether that's in a networking group, or whether it's in a business, in a professional networking group that's quite formal, and I've seen people in a meltdown to the point where I think you do need some support, but I don't think this group is the right place for that to happen for you.

And it's knowing where is the right place to go. Is that more one-to-one support? Is it a different type of challenge or whatever that they need, etc.? So, definitely, that's something that -- and there are others that just have been afraid to ask anyone to help them, and they just are mottled, and it's a shame because their business has been a good one, but it's just lost legs as they've struggled with it.

Paul: Is there one thing that you wish you'd known when you started?

Is there something that, you wish you could tell Val on day one of the business, hey, just remember this, or just think about this? Is there anything that stands out for that?

Val: Oh, gosh, just one thing? Can I have two?

Paul: Have as many as you need...

Val: Because one is a really practical thing, get the right hardware. When I started my business, I bought a laptop and I had a mobile phone, and that was it. So, initially, it was I've got to get a website, I've got to get a website, I've got to do that. And I did that first. And I still think it's the best thing for me, the best investment ever, in the supoort, was but it was finding the right person at the beginning of my business, who's still with me, to help me develop my website, build my website, to work it with me, still doing some more work with that to redo it and everything. Who, actually, has been more than a web developer. It's not a techy person, that is what they do, as well, but it's somebody who was around from the beginning. And I think somebody should have said to me at the beginning, spend more resource and energy in investing in that, in the support rather than actually buying bits of kit that somebody told you that you needed.

So rather than the laptop that I spent a lot of money on because I went into a shop and they said, you need all of this stuff. Get some advice about what your type of business will, actually, need before you start spending money. And I've heard that from lots of different types of businesses, get some good advice at the outset before you spend money. I spent lots of money, now I look back, advertising in all sorts of publications that just weren't my target market at all, and, really, now I look back, and I think, why was I at that place? That's not my market.

And, actually, if I could speak to myself then, I would say, "Keep all of that money because you're going to need that in year three, you're going to need that in year four." And I think having a sound bit of support and advice at the beginning. My money would have probably been better spent, I have to say, Paul, in some good business coaching or marketing development program, or something that was, actually, about developing you as a business owner and not buying bits of stuff and paying for advertising and whatever, I think. Does that help?

Paul: Yes. The first thing I bought when I started and I've not thought about until now. The first thing I bought when I started a business was a small handheld video camera to collect testimonials. I didn't have any clients. I had no way of getting clients. At no point had I thought about getting clients. But I thought, should I have a client, I'll need to capture a testimonial on video. Yeah. It's funny those decisions that you take at the start. I think the point of having someone from as early as possible in your world, in your business, to guide you would have been massive. I think absolutely it would have been massive.

Val: I think, definitely and I guess why I was mentioning the thing about the laptop specifically is that I came from quite a corporate environment and background. I was a lawyer. Yes, I was in local government, and then I was in a large sort of education college, but, ultimately, it's public sector, it's corporate, and what I think I took from that to my business -- there were lots of great things that I took from that to my business, but one of the things I took that I tried hard to kind of shake away, I think, is the kind of corporate I've got to analyse everything to the end before you make any decision and move on.

But, also, I bought that laptop with a full Office suite or whatever, Outlook and Excel and whatever, even before I knew what I was going to use it for because that's what I'd always had. I don't use Outlook now. No disrespect to anybody who does, but you don't need to pay for that type of mail package to run my business. I need other things, but it isn't that. But at the beginning, I spent my money, very quickly, and it was dead money, really, because I couldn't use it.

Paul: On similar, is there one thing or a couple things that you'd do differently if you could do it all again? Is there one sort of big thing that you'd like to have done or just you wish you'd started to do earlier?

Val: Yeah. I think the starting to do earlier for me, I think the networking thing. I did quite a lot of that in my old jobs, and I continue with that and I love it, and I think I do it well, and other things. But I think much earlier, saying no to things.

Which is interesting because then, again, don't get me wrong. I still find myself saying yes when I think, really, should I stop and maybe I should have said no, and I think I'm better at it now, but wish I had started to say no to things, some things earlier. Because now I've got a few examples where I've said no, more confidently, and it's been a better decision for the business.

And being more confident to actually say, "This is what I do. What you've asked me to do will cost you this, and that's the price," and not actually, when they come back and say, "Oh, that's too expensive and it's out of our budget. Can you do something on the price?" Not saying, "Okay. I can knock 10% off." Because that, ultimately, says you're not worth the original thing.

And I say, I think, definitely, that is a looking-back thing, actually, not find yourself in situations where you're underpricing or underselling or under-promoting what you do and the skills that you bring, I think.

Paul: And talking about business and growth and moving it forward, what has been the most potent strategy? What's the thing that you've done that you think has had the biggest effect on moving your business forward?

Val: Being completely honest about what you are and what you're not as a business. I hope it doesn't sound too simplistic, but I've kept that all the way through. When I speak to key people about what I do, I generally tell them, this is what I do. If I haven't done something before that they're asking me to do, I'll say, "I've not done that before; however, I do have experience in this, and I think I will be able to do what you're asking me to do" But I never pretend to be something that I'm not. I keep learning and giving credit to other people. If I see something that you're doing that I think looks great, I'll lift the phone, drop you an email, tweet you, whoever you're are and say, "That looks amazing." That's given me a lot of ideas, or I found that very interesting.

As opposed to, well, that looks great. I think I'll copy that, and do that. I try really hard not to be that kind of business. And I say that to clients, I want them to make the best decision if they want to book me as their wedding planner, as their mentor, as their event planner, then that's great, but I also want them to make the right decision for them.

So if I feel that what they're looking for isn't something that I can offer them that's the best for them, then I'll say that, which can be hard because firstly, you're saying, you're pushing them away to somebody else. But I want them to be the right fit I want to be the right choice for them.

Paul: What would be the biggest bit of advice for the guys we know that have all the attributes to make it but just feel like they are swimming in the dark.

Val: I'd say not to rush things, or to be impatient in terms of how long things actually can take before you get a great outcome. But I don't mean put off, hesitate, procrastinate. It's not the same thing, in my mind. I think being confident to set yourself some realistic goals, but, also, make sure they're challenging enough for you. Everybody, I think, knows what their level is, so is this right for me, there are people who will take high risks. I know somebody last year who did just that. It was a high-risk decision made. They researched it and they took that risk. I personally would not have taken that risk, but they were comfortable with it.

You've got to know your own risk appetite, I guess, for want of a better word. And if you're comfortable with that and you've looked into itand it's right for you and your business, never mind what someone else is doing, it's right for you and your business, then you take that decision.

I would, also, say, and I think you said this to me before, as well, Paul, sometimes, actually, what's the worst that can happen? You try something and it doesn't work. Well, then, you learn from it. You refine it, and then do something different next time. There are lots of amazing businesses who've made mistakes along the way. There's something about saying to somebody, you know what, that didn't work, so that's why we're not doing it like this again, and we've learned loads from it. We're now a better business as a result of learning from that mistake. Everyone makes them. It's whether you learn from them as to whether you're good or not, I think.

Paul: It's a really good point. As a finishing thing, we're back to single things, is there a strategy you've employed or maybe that has made the biggest difference?

Val: I think it is confidence and honesty because I think if you can confidently be honest with yourself and your decisions, you will have the business you want to have. I guess as a wedding planner, my decision, in respect to weddings, is that I don't want to be somebody who has every weekend throughout the year or throughout the main season on a wedding. I'd rather have fewer, more detailed, and fine contacts, if that makes sense.

In wedding industry, there are lots of people talking about how many jobs they've got if you ask a florist how many weddings they have this month, the figure will scare you, and if you ask a photographer how many weddings they have booked in next year, that figure may scare you because they may have 50 and I may have chosen to have 6 and if you don't have the confidence to do what you honestly want to do, it easy to feel you are not successful, I'm not doing well.

What you need to do if you want to have a comparison, again, I think you should compare to what you're aiming for, not someone else. But if you say, actually, as a business, I want X amount in my business next year. To bring that in, I will need to do whatever it is. That's the way you should do. Not, well, that person said that they're doing 20, and I'm only doing seven, so, oh, my God, I'm not doing very well. I think you do have to be honest about the sort of business that you're running.

I want to be personally involved in all these events, so, therefore, I'm only doing that number. That's what you, really, want to do.

Paul: It's so personal, I think your business is about the most personal thing you can have because it doesn't need to do anything other than what you want it to do. And we see so many people that I almost feel are living someone else's business dream because they're trying to achieve this goal that actually they don't really want. It's sad, and it's painful. It can take something that is, while it's challenging, massively fulfiling, and kind of strip the enjoyment out of it.

Val: Yeah, definitely. I think I'm saying if you find yourself living somebody else's dream, then that goes back to how it was if you used to work for an organisation, and you were living someone else's dream then, and you said you wanted to set up your business not to do that, why are you now in your own business trying to borrow somebody else's strategy or plan or idea? Where are your own? Develop your own. Make sure this is your business.

Once upon a time

Once upon a time ...

People like stories not things. We are taught right from childhood to delve into our imaginations and disappear into stories. Multi-million pound block buster movies and book successes, such as Harry Potter, shows us just how popular stories are.

Stories can by hypnotic. They slip from the conscious to the sub-concious mind. They let us experience many emotions and never feel 'salesy'. Creating a riveting story related to your target market can be an extremely powerful tool to communicate your message and persuade your prospects.

What do you go home and share with your family and friends "you'll never guess what happened today at work...."?

The interesting, people filled stories you tell over a beer...."we worked with this business and the owner has just bought a new all-singing yacht and met x celebrity on their first sail...." "The new teeth we helped create have meant one of our clients has been on a date for the first time in twelve years...".

What stories can you introduce into your marketing? You can make yourself the subject of your story and your family (giving your business personality and likeability); it could be about a member of your team (awards, exams, how they helped a client and the impact of that); embellish testimonials with the full story; include case studies and feedback. People love 'rags to riches', underdog type of tales.

We remember stories. Some of the best comedians use stories to take us on a journey...do the same throughout your marketing.

Incorporate stories into your
- sales letters
- web copy,
- emails
- brochures
- blogs
- brochures
- blogs

...in fact anywhere your prospects can read about you and your business.

Your business ethos and strong selling messages will be subliminally hidden in your stories making it near-on impossible for would-be clients to forget or ignore you.

The End.

Give them a good reason to leave their email address

Give them a good reason to leave their email address

You will be advised time and time again to 'build a list' of your target audience so that you can take control of the marketing conversation.

One way to build that list is by offering something called a 'Lead Bait'. A tantalising morsel of help, information or inspiration that will be so irresistible your potential clients will be eager to leave their email address in exchange for your magnet.

So what you dangle as an offering has to be relevant to what you do and help identify prospects needing your service or product.

That is its only purpose.

A lead bait simply gets people to raise their hands and say "I'm interested."

What is happening here is attraction marketing. You are attracting like a magnet a group of prospects.

Whether you are a dentist, a mortgage broker or a marketer...in fact whatever your sector or niche there will be a lead magnet within your business.

"10 ways to keep your teeth pristine white"

"What questions you should ask any mortgage lender before your sign"

"9 Mistakes of email marketing every business owner should avoid"

Examples of lead baits include:-

- Free reports
- PDF report or White paper download
- Free book
- MPS3 audio transcript
- Privileged access to videos

Any of these or even a combination of them works well. Books have a particularly high-perceived value, establishing you as an expert.

Once you have the email address and name of a potential client your marketing can really begin. Lead magnets are the beginning of a 'courting ' process from where you can gently build a relationship of trust.

Book bonus available here:
www.marketingjumpleads.com/game-changer-book-bonuses

Second bite of the cherry

Second bite of the cherry
- bonus of Facebook Retargeting Videos

Making a sale is a process.

Studies have shown that up to 98% of your visitors leave your website without converting. Your savvy, discerning customer will now take several steps (according to Google sometimes up to x30!) before deciding to buy from your business.

Retargeting helps you tackle this problem head on.

It allows you to target and serve ads only to people who've previously visited your website, used your mobile app, or in some cases, previously bought from you.

This means you can be very strategic and efficient about who you're reaching and where you're spending your marketing budget.

Retargeting gives you a 'second bite of the cherry'. You can send highly targeted ads to exactly the right people.

Put simply, retargeting is one of the most powerful ways to re-engage with your audience and get more sales. It is an incredible way to grow your business on auto-pilot. Interestingly, almost certainly your competitors won't be thinking this way.

You are simply going back to an audience that already 'knows' your business on some level and sharing a targeted ad. You will have experienced this yourself. Have you ever been on a website and looked at pair of shoes or holiday cottage, only to see that same pair of shoes or cottage in Facebook ads or web pages you subsequently visit, following you around.

You have been 're-targeted' with something you've browsed before. In effect you've put up your hand to say I may be interested in those shoes, or booking that event or cottage.

The science and psychology is easy to understand. If you keep seeing that great pair of shoes, you probably meant to buy, but life 'got busy', eventually you'll be prompted and reminded enough to drag out your wallet and make the purchase, or book the event or whatever desired action would be great for the business posting the 'retargeting ads'.

We'd all like to think that every single person that comes in contact with our business follows a very straight and orderly path to buying our products and services. Someone visits our site for the first time, then fills out a form to download this Game Changers ebook, then is interested in trialling Marketing Jumpleads, all in one session on our website. Minutes later, they complete the sign-up form, hand over their credit card details to become a fully signed up member (it does happen...but rarely!)

In reality, our buyer's journey is probably not so linear. People pop over to our website then leave. Two months later, they discover our latest blog article, and then decide to download a 'cheat sheet'. A few days after that, they decide to check out another blog post or read a LinkedIn article. Maybe a week later they decide to get in touch about coming to a local meeting, and it takes several more weeks of meetings and discussions to come to a decision to buy and join. Same end result, but the process is a little more convoluted!

So marketers need to be prepared to help their buyers through that convoluted process. Retargeting ads are your way of managing, analysing (and tweaking) and speeding up this journey.

We're calling retargeting the 'magic sauce' that gives every size business an unprecedented opportunity.

It's not hard to do. It's easier to set-up than you think. The results are a real game-changer.

Book Bonus available here:
Facebook Retargeting Videos
How to set-up & manage Facebook retargeting
www.marketingjumpleads.com/game-changer-book-bonuses

Julia Roberts *MarketingJumpLeads*

Julia is a true, serial, Entrepreneur who brings over 22 years of hands-on expe- rience of the trials and tribulations of running her own businesses. Bubbling with enthusiasm and full of ideas, Julia is great at creating the 'journey through your business'.

www.marketingjumpleads.com

Paul: So – business partner....I know why I do it. Why do you -- what's it really about for you? Why are you doing this thing? Why are you running a business yourself? Why not doing it for someone else?

Julia: Well, it's definitely changed. When I first started, I wanted to run a huge, million pound business. It was all financial dreams when I first started. Now, it's much more about being in control, I'm completely in control of my own time, I choose who I get to work with, and we work with some fantastic people. It's about a lifestyle. It's about a way of working. I wonder if I'm almost unemployable now because I've been doing it for way too long, 25 years plus. I couldn't have to be at a certain office at a certain time. That just wouldn't fit anymore.

So, definitely, freedom. Freedom of choices. Also, and it sounds a bit pretentious, but I really, really enjoy helping our members and our clients. I love it when it all comes together, when we, you can see how the marketing is working for them. I love that. There's definitely highs and lows running a business, and the highs well exceed, well out-balance any lows. So it's about lifestyle and time, and it's about giving back and really seeing the good work that you're doing.

Paul: So with that in mind then, if that's the point of it, what does success look like for you? How do you know that the work you've put into it has been worth it?

Julia: I am here to earn money. I do want a lifestyle. I do want a certain way of living. So there is a definite financial goals. We're doing really well on that. So we've got definite goals, and I think that real, "tangible goal is vital. I've made lots of mistakes along the way, and I didn't have a clear plan. I was definitely getting in my car, and not having a map and knowing where I was driving to. So I always dreamed that someday I would earn X grand a month, but never had a clear plan to do that. Definitely, we have that in place now in our business. We know where we're going and what we want to do.

So there is a financial goal. But I also want to enjoy my day, what I do and who I work with. I love working with you, Paul. And that enjoyment is a massively important part of my working life. I love the clients that we work with and the members that we have. Spending time with the right people.

I don't get up and think, oh, it's Monday and it's work. I get up, and I'm looking forward to tweaking a campaign or looking forward to making something really work and making some social media, actually earn money for the business that we're working with. So success is, definitely, enjoying the hours, and often, we know as business owners that is many hours, but actually getting up and enjoying my day. I know we're helping other businesses grow at the same time we're growing ours. I feel part of something really exciting, and that, for me, is success.

Paul: You have to enjoy the journey, especially smaller businesses, you have to enjoy the journey or enjoy the thing you're doing. If you're just looking for the result, you're in the wrong place, I think.

Julia: And I think, if I am honest, I was there myself, definitely, for too long. I, definitely, just had this kind of pie-in-the-sky idea of where I wanted to get to without a clear path. It was just drudgery. I was a busy fool for probably over a decade, well over a decade, just running around. I wasn't having holidays because I was working all the time, and I thought it would come good just because I was working so hard, which was just nonsense. I sort of felt I deserved it, and it would, somehow, come if I just kept battering away, but I had no clear path. So, the clarity is a big learning curve for a business owner, and that's, definitely, what we've got now. I haven't always had that, and that's a big piece of success.

Paul: I think with the things you've done before, and certainly now, why do you think you have done so well?

Julia: Definitely hard work. Now, it's working because it's focused hard work. So I know exactly where we want to get to. So it's a definite roadmap in terms of numbers, and growth, and all those kind of things. But I've learned how to do it. I think most businesses are set up based on a passion or an interest, at least, in a subject. I had a chain of beauty salons for many years, and I had an interest in that area. But I never learned how to be a business owner.

The key, the thing that's radically changed, I mean, unbelievable difference, is I learnt to learn how to do the marketing. So I learned how to attract quality customers as opposed to any customer. For years and years, I just reacted. It was like I was spinning plates. There was always one or two toppling off, and I ran between them all, just being this busy fool. Then I learned how to do the marketing. So I was spending my time wisely, attracting the right kind of customers to come into the salons, and we, basically, doubled our turnover, but went from five salons to one. It just made all the difference. I learned how to do it well. I properly got to understand and learned one or two key skills that now set me up every day for what I do.

Paul: So it may be linked then, on the other side of that, why do you think the majority of business owners struggle or, ultimately, fail?

Julia: I think because when they set up they are very good at the things they come into the business for. So they're good at arranging flowers, mending cars, setting up IT programs. But there are a huge range of skills you have to be as a business owner. I've been everything from a counselor IT support, the HR department, through to the finances.

Most businesses fail, and this is certainly my failing in my first years in business is I tried to do it all myself. Under a false economy, I thought that I could do it all myself, I was saving money. In fact, I was costing myself so much money and so much time because I didn't get the right help in.

So I didn't hang around with a lot of people. I didn't have the right expertise. I was trying to run my accounts, doing laundry for seven salons, all that. Just ridiculous when I look back now. But I always thought that once it got good, then I would pay to have those things done.

I think we hold on. It was my baby, and it was letting go and letting other people do some of it felt enormous. I didn't do that quick enough. So I didn't surround myself with the right support or get the right help, and I think that's why most businesses fail.

That and monetary cash, really understanding your numbers and the cash flow. It's so important to really understand them. It's very easy to come up with all the great ideas and all the things you could do. There's too much choice almost. Especially in the marketing world, there's so many things you can do, and for entrepreneurs it's easy to focus on the new and shiny things and we don't stop to work out if the business I actually running properly. Now I'm systemised. I've got the right people around me to make sure that they're being done. The things I'm not good at or used to put off such as the accounts is now done by someone who does it much better than I ever could and much quicker and in the right way. So it's surrounding yourself with the right help, outsource or employ way quicker than you think you should. That's definitely the big change for me.

Paul: I think you probably answered a bit of it, but is there a thing, one thing that you wish you'd known when you started?

Julia: Well, I think, and I'm going to say this because we are a marketing business, but I think you should learn how to do your marketing. I think you really need to understand how to find and keep more customers. It's the lifeblood, and it's often the first thing that gets dropped from spend if there is a downturn in the economy or things get tight. Actually, it's the one thing you should be spending the most on all of the time consistently.

You need to have marketing that is always running for your business and always bringing in leads, contacts, and then a way of converting those into sales. Often business owners are not born with those skills but you also can't use that as an excuse if you don't know how to do it, then find someone to do it who is good and gives you a proper return for the money that you're spending. But you've got to have the marketing running. When I first started I didn't have that. I just reacted. When we went quiet, I'd suddenly throw out an offer. It was all offer based and it wasn't a consistent

Paul: I do really find it interesting that so few new businesses put any thought and especially cash into how to get some customers. They design something beautiful and they put all their effort into it and have no idea and no way of finding out who is actually going to buy it. I remember in particular a stunning hotel, beautifully hidden away, incredibly nice inside, but the people that set it up just put all their money into making the perfect product, and then, virtually, went under because they had no money left to find people to fill it. So they ended up with this beautiful hotel sat empty and massive pile of frustration and debt. I think this is, particularly with people right at that startup, save some cash, as much as you think you can, more than you probably think you need, save some cash to go and find customers.

Julia: Yeah. It's going for it, and also I just believed that if I set up this stunning salon, and we gave great service, that word of mouth, and people would come. It doesn't work like that. Certainly, not anymore. It was easy when I set up. It was Yellow Pages and a few leaflets, and we were busy because we were the only ones around.

The choice for all of our customers now is enormous. Our customers have got more discerning so they are more aware. At their fingertips, they can find 20 alternatives to your business. So you have to stand out, and so you have to work really hard to attract the right kind of customers.   You can be the best restaurant in town, you could give the best financial advice, you can be the top of your trade. Someone who's good at marketing will always do better than you because they are finding the people and telling their story. So it is that simple. It is a lesson that took me many years to learn.

Paul: It's true know lots of people with rubbish products that sell loads of stuff because they're good at the sale.

And we have people with beautiful, great, well-thought-out products that are going out of business because they haven't put any time and effort into the only thing you need, which is just some customers.

So I think you probably have answered it but if you could do it all over again, what would you do differently?

Julia: In a way, I've been privileged because I've set up a salon business, made a lot of the mistakes and then I have been able to set up again with Marketing JumpLeads. So we've been able to put in a proper system. We've got a good CRM system. A lot of all the lessons and things I wish I'd done before we've now put into place.

Yes we could all do more marketing. We could always do more. That's a big lesson. It was a huge thing is that your to-do list is never going to be empty, and if it is, then you're not pushing yourself enough, you're not growing. Accept you're always going to have things on your list. Somehow once I got that concept, then life became a little easier.

So I'm never going to have done it all, but I know I'm doing way more than most of my competitors are. I'm always trying to improve it and always working through it. But you have to let yourself off. I think that I would put systems in place and get more help sooner. I know I can't do it all myself anymore.

Paul: Our big finish, our final question and obviously this is what we actually do, but if you were going to look at a business owner and just give them one bit of advice, what would it be?

Julia: To consistently have a system to attract new customers and leads and to keep existing customers really excited and enthusiastic about you. That is a proper system. Not just relying on word of mouth.

A proper systemised mechanism in your business day in, day out, that is finding you new potential customers and keeping your existing customers happy. If you can get that properly sorted, it's the most exciting thing. It's the panacea for a new business really. It opens up all of the opportunities for you, and once it is running you have a business you can amplify. Yes, you'll change it now and again, yes, you'll need to keep tweaking it, but overall, it is a little machine that keeps your business vibrant and new people coming to find you. If that's happening, then you can concentrate on what you're good at, and you can concentrate on looking after your team and bringing in the right customers.

Paul: I think the interesting thing about the systemised bit is that it doesn't need to be some clever online, find them on Facebook, walk them through different steps automatically system.   It really more of a consistent way of doing it. We know plenty of businesses that are just drop out a hundred postcards through doors, they normally get 2 clients per hundred So that's their thing, and that happens every month.

All they have to do is find another hundred doors. But they do every single month do that because they know it works.

Julia: I think it's consistency. But most businesses that we deal with and me myself for too many years, I was, like I said, reactive, and I'd do some things and it'd stop because we got busy again. It's consistency of doing that that's the key to success. Whatever that looks like and whatever it is for you. Like I say, online, offline, simplistic cards to fancy sales forms, it doesn't matter. Whatever works in your space, have it set up week in, week out it's happening so to find the right people.

Look for the money in your sector

Look for the money in your sector

Do you want your business to be positioned as Easyjet or Virgin? Skoda or Mercedes? All good business models in their own right, but it can be far easier to find the decent returns in the affluent arenas.

Some sectors, in particular, seem to have been hit hard by the economic downturn and the natural reaction is cut prices. Any price cutting 'war' can simply be a race to the bottom and failure.

Could you look to sell primarily to higher earners or affluent business sectors? Those who are willing to pay premium prices in return for expertise, service and experiences.

This is the fastest and safe route to prosper in tough times as this audience is least affected by economic challenges. The even better news, there is an explosion of demand for premium service. Spending in the luxury end of the market is on the up, across the board. How can you business tap into that?

This shift in spending behaviour is concentrated in a minority – but a very powerful minority. Best of all it is easy to identify WHO they are, WHAT they desire and WHAT they respond to. If you can tap into this sector you can profit well.

If you run a 'earn by the hour' business such as a hairdresser or dentist you can look really busy, with appointments booked weeks ahead, but are the bookings with your ideal clients? Ones that will cherish your premium package and pay you what your skills are worth?

Don't get in to a price battle to the bottom, instead aim for the top 20% of your market who control the majority of the spending. It's easier, often more enjoyment and you won't be affected by economic fluctuations.

Take people offline as soon as possible

Take people off-line as soon as possible

One of the key practices we talk about (and will keep talking about!) is the importance of building a list of people who are interested in what you do.

Pulling people in from online channels is one of the best ways of doing this. Offering people value from social media, via your web pages in return for their email address is the easiest way of doing this and should be a constant focus of your business.

But it mustn't stop there.

If you are solely engaging with them in the "online world, it is harder to keep their attention, as they are only ever a few movements of the hand away from your competitors, and you miss a big trick in appearing to them when they are "in their own time".

A recent survey suggested that over 60% of consumers pay more attention to the mail that lands through their letterbox than they do to the email that arrives in their inbox – so if you JUST send emails you are going to be missing out on a good proportion of the prospects.

Don't get me wrong doing it online is much better than doing nothing, but with figures like the above, not at least testing off-line strategies is a big mistake.

Take the example of newsletters. Newsletters are a really useful tool to get into a client's consciousness, position you as the expert and build a relationship. But for them to really work they need to be read, and when are they most likely to be read?

When they drop in your inbox, often in the working day with a stack of other emails to be read, or when it arrives direct to your letter box for you to enjoy at your leisure, in your down time. Unless your competitors are delivering a newsletter at exactly the same time – you will also get their undivided attention.

Hard printed copy is good for trust, good for credibility and the reality is that most of your competitors won't think it is cost effective.

So as you are building your list getting customers online, find an excuse to take them offline. Is there a book, or a report, or guide you can physically send them?

Make them the offer, ask them for their address and send something. Your message will arrive in their space when they have time to see it and think about it.

Book bonus available here:
www.marketingjumpleads.com/game-changer-book-bonuses

The secret to getting more done

The secret to getting more done

You know that feeling that you have so much to do but don't know where to start – so don't anything?

Yes you do and so does every other business owner on the planet. Procrastination is a killer of small businesses.

So how do some people crack through it and grow their business whilst other get bogged down and just grow their to-do list?

Two BIG Secrets.

1) You will never get it all done. Ever. There will always be something to do, the list will not end. Successful business owners understand this and consequently don't even try to empty the do list because they know it is futile and a waste of precious energy. They focus on the important stuff and stop waiting time on the rest.

2) If you don't have a really clear picture of where you are trying to get to you will NEVER get there.

Really successful business owner have a beyond crystal clear picture of where they are going. What money they are going to make, from what projects involving how many clients, in how much time. They know when they want to work and when they will be off. Consequently they can start at their end goal and work everything back from that end point to build a list of steps they need to take to get them there.

So for anything that comes up in their business, they can run it by the question,

"Is this getting me close to where I want to get to?"

If the answer is "yes" – they do it,If the answer is "no" they avoid, delegate it or out source it.

Everyone has got the same amount of time, and at the risk of stating the obvious, it's how you use it that will be the key to your success.

There will always be so much to do, but you need to cut yourself some slack. Realise that you are not going to get it all done and so you may as well focus on the critical stuff that gets you close to where you want to be.

But of course if you don't know that fundamental end point you can't do anything... better get those plans mapped out.

Book bonus available here:
www.marketingjumpleads.com/game-changer-book-bonuses

Liam Nash *ChapmanAssociates*

Liam Nash is Chartered Financial Planner running his business out of Melton Mowbray in the East Midlands.
Starting as the 'teaboy' at 16 he worked his way up through one company in West Yorkshire, where he was born and bred, moving on to Chapman Associates which he bought into and subsequently sold to a FTSE 100 company 7 years later. Along with his business partner their new LLP is consistently ranked in the highest performers in its location within St. James's Place.

His moto for business is if you ever lose, don't lose the lesson. Oh yeah and mines a Guinness
http://www.chapman-associates.co.uk/

Paul: It's about you rather than what you do as business. Why are you doing this as a business owner as opposed to doing it for someone else, being part of someone else's team?

Liam: I think the main reason it ended up like that was that I just realised I could do it better than anybody else.

I realised I could do it better than anybody else, I thought! Therefore, I could change anything I wanted to whenever I wanted to. But I didn't go into it all on my own. I've always had business partners. I've always thought that you need somebody to bounce ideas off and to hold you back when you got an idea that potentially might be a bit too dangerous or a little bit too exciting for the real world.

So I've always had a business partner, and long may that continue. I don't think I want to go out alone. For me that's having someone within the business, for others you might need just a business group to share ideas with and put those kind of things to. When you get excited about something, sometimes you don't see the obvious hurdle.

Paul: I do. I think really with lot's of business I do genuinely think loneliness, almost in a non-emotional way and emotionally too is just really difficult. It's the idea of having people to bounce off. But it's particularly as a new business, trying to do it all on your own and hold it all in your own head I think it's a big reason why a lot of businesses fail because they don't have people around them.

Liam: That's true.

Paul: The problem with business partners, I think it's really hard to find a good one if you don't know them well. It's really easy to find, get excited, find a bad one, and the try to extricate yourself.

Liam: Yeah. It's the one bit from the original days. I've been self-employed for probably 20 years now. But even though I was self-employed, I was with a group of people. There's our administration teams that help out. There was a business owner of that practice. You were with a group of people even though you were sort of paddling your own canoe, or whatever silly phrase you want to use. You ultimately have people to talk to, people to work with who might give you different ideas.

Like I said, from a business partner point of view you could walk away at any point because I was self employed in a business if that makes sense, So it was pretty free. But, yes, good business partners are hard to come by.

Paul: So what does success look like for you?. How do you know it's happening? What does the world look like when you've "made it"? How do you know that what you've been through the last 20 years has been worth it?

Liam: I think you really relate it to money and being in that game, and it probably is related to money, but is also sort of not true. But it makes things an awful lot easier when you've got money. In our business we try and get everybody what we class as financially independent, which mean a result for what you've worked for and what you've worked towards, you've got enough cash or business that's generating enough income for it to pay your bills. Everybody in the world wants that. It doesn't matter how big your bills are. Everybody's desire is that the amount of money that comes in is more than the amount of money that goes out.

So success, to me, is that the hassle or the distraction of that disappears. Because it can consume you, and every single day is thinking about trying to earn an honest crust to pay the bills distracts you from being able to do what you are good at or what you can focus on.

So taking away that focus or taking away that distraction means you can focus on creating the nice things in your business, the things that need a bit of investment, either monetary wise or time wise, where you're not, actually, generating an income. You're not worried anymore. It means you can go off and be a little bit off the wall or take time to develop and work on your business rather than in it. Which is often the stuff that gives you stability.

Oddly on a Monday morning, there are not many people queuing up for a pension strategy.

So I try and go out and generate that residual. It's difficult work and a lot of hard work. But if you can get the money coming in on a regular basis from clients that have committed to you longer term, then it means that you don't expect or have to go out and find somebody a new pension to get paid on. There's enough income coming in. You can improve your service to them. I think that goes back to income. So I'm measuring success in income. I probably tell everybody that that's not everything. I advise them that money's not a measure of success, but it is when you start out.

Paul: Yeah, I think so. I think it has to be there. It's something as a business owner you have to be honest with yourself both ways. I'm not struggling to be a multimillionaire because I don't want to do what it takes. I want a lifestyle from it. But for all those folk that say money's not important, you do need it. Without it, not only does it make life actually quite difficult, it makes doing the stuff that you really want to do less likely to happen because you're stressing about the next bill, the next bill, the next bill.

Liam: It's a great world to think that you're not after money, but, eventually, as people start taking your furniture away if you don't pay, it's money.

Paul: Looking at what you do, why do you think you've done so well? By any measure, you look at your lifestyle, look at your success, look at your freedom that you have, why have you done so well? What do you point that towards?

Liam: I break up with girls a lot because then I get miserable and spend more time in the office because there's no one else to look after. Yes. So a lot of self sacrifice

Liam: What was the question?

Paul: Why do you think you've done so well. Can you look back and pull something out that you think has made the difference?

Liam: I think, ultimately, I know and believe that they couldn't get better advice anywhere else that was genuinely designed for them. Yes, there's some creative stuff in there. That means that we get paid. But, ultimately, if I don't get paid, I know that next time I will. So I don't do it directly to benefit me day one. It's, ultimately, client focused. It's always on their outcomes, and if I can find a way to get paid in between times, even better.

Paul: So paraphrasing, is it about having a purpose beyond the service, it's more about how you do what you do rather than any product deliver? Is that that right?

Liam: I think it's just that we take a very complicated or potentially complicated area, convert it into something that's not complicated because nobody needs to know the 16 different pension regimes to understand what a pension is fundamentally.

We try and simplify it as best we can. We answer any questions that people ask if they want a bit more detail. But, ultimately, they trust in us because we wouldn't be advising that course of action if we truly didn't believe in it, one, because we have to put it in writing. It's pretty much guaranteed to be right because I don't put anything in writing that isn't right.

So they come to me as a professional. I give them some professional advice. If they don't want to take it, then they go and find somebody to fulfill that action. I think that the difficult part to explain is all our experience, if I believe it's the right thing for them to do, then we're going to do it. It's not because I want to sell a product we're doing it because it's the right thing to do, and we've built a relationship based on our results so why wouldn't our clients take our advice?

Paul: So how can you be so sure. What have you done in the last 20 years that has put you in the position to where you can take all that information that they give you and kind of distill it into the right course of action? Is it just time on the job? Is it extra learning?

Liam: No, I think time on the job is a little different, but I do I think experience is key. My dad told me once a story I loved, which was that you can have 20 years' experience, or you can have one year's experience 20 times over.

I think you've got to learn from every single day, you can't be pretending that you know stuff. Because 20 years ago you might think that you knew everything, but the day after it's changed, it's altered. You can't just pretend that you've learned it all 20 years ago, and everything is going to be brilliant.

You've got to be open and realistic. You're learning every single day. You'll have some experiences of what went badly and what went well and a gut instinct that links it all together. But, ultimately, you just got to be aware that you've always got to be continuously growing and educating yourself.

Paul: What do you think you have done differently from the majority of the people?

Liam: I think lots of people blame stuff that you can't do anything about. So we've ignored that. Such as the stock market falling and Brexit mess or that you had the recession. It's going to happen. So what? I can't do anything about it. What's the point in wasting time in thinking about it? You can only feel one certain way every day, and I just think I prefer to feel happy. There's a belief that we can get out of it, so we'll go straight through it, rather than believing that the world's against us and we can't. As soon as you start believing like that, then it's a self-fulfilling prophecy.

Paul: Following on from that, maybe it would be the same for them. Why do you think for business owners as a whole, struggle or fail?

Liam: They probably give up a bit too early. They might just be on the verge of everything clicking into place and being right, and they just throw their hands up and give up a little bit too early. My focus is always on the result I'm driving towards. I think in fact, this is human nature. If you are stuck a traffic jam and you want to get to Halifax, for example...

I'd prefer to be constantly moving and traveling away from that destination rather than sat where in a massive queue because it's the shortest distance to get to Halifax.

I want to constantly be moving, and that's the difference, all I care about is getting to Halifax. I prefer to be moving and I'll keep trying different ways to get there. Whatever that blockage is, or whatever it is, it could be a massive pile up that's going to be there for two hours or two days. I prefer to be going elsewhere than figuring it out. We focus on the destination or the result, not ignoring everything else, but ultimately, if I have to travel twice as far to get to that result, then I'll travel twice as far. I'll work twice as hard or remove a barrier, jump over it.

Paul: So looking back then, tell me when you first started self-employed, if you could have told that 16-year-old something, just a thing to keep in mind as he steps out on his journey, what would it be?

Liam: What's the biggest thing I've learned? Literally, that hard work is, ultimately, all you ever know, like a friend of mine told me. When you're young, you haven't got experience, you haven't got knowledge. The only way you're going to find it is to learn it and spend more time doing it, I think the self-employed side of it sort of dropped on me at the time because of circumstances, but I never looked back. I'm now in charge of my own destiny, and I'm going to make sure that I get there.

What would I tell myself now? Promise myself not to do some of the silly things I did. It's not related to business.

Liam: I'd drink less. I did say it wasn't directly busines related! I do know that had I fulfilled one of my promises to myself, that I'd be an awful lot more wealthy now than I am, and I'm still regretful for it. If I didn't drink and let's just say I was a little bit more healthy, that the amount of times that I've spent hung over could have been used more fruitfully.

So whether it's self-development or life skills and stuff I did say to myself that if I quit drinking until I hit a million quid, I know that I'd have got to be a millionaire quicker than doing it the way I did.

Paul: So if you could do your business over again, what would you do differently?

Liam: I'd employ people quicker. I'd invest in more people quicker. I'd probably think about the sort of induction of those people and the training of people to make it a little bit more planned.

Lots of people think, oh, I need some new employees because people start telling me that they were understaffed and stuff. Then you bring them in, and then for the first week they just shadow people, just teling them to do this and that and you'll pick it up. I think you just miss out on a real good opportunity to start off from day one to get somebody skilled up as quickly as you possibly can.

So if you're ever going to take somebody on, have a proper plan. Even from 9:00 in the morning when they first join you all the way through to the first day of going to the kitchen and making the cups of tea and buying your cake.

It's having a full structured day, tell them the story of the business, tell them how the business works, and give them all the background that they need and try to interlink it all. Because bringing somebody in just because you can afford to employ them, which most people never think they can, but you can, and to get them quickly trained up is the best investment of time and effort. Because they can just do all the stuff that you don't like doing. Look for what they are good at if they have a particular desire to do a job or responsibility look out for it.

So if they love following up clients just to update them on stuff because they just enjoy talking to people, then that job's given to that individual. Because there's no point getting one of the people that don't really like talking to clients to phone them because they're not enjoying it. I think it comes across in the voice. They won't get it right and so they won't improve it any better than we've currently got.

Whereas, if you've got a desire, you can continuously improve on what you've got in place, and get it to a place where it gets that efficient that it doesn't need you. It's brilliant. Then you just go find somebody else to do it. But most business owners have still got the job mentality. They don't like doing that. They think that the job will be gone if they're too efficient.

Paul: So when it comes to actual growth is there one strategy that you can point to and say, that's what we've done, or it's something you can go back to relying on?

Liam: I think it's different for us more recently because we've taken on two new advisors similar to us, and they're starting out on their own. We've realised that we just keep on saying it'll come and just work hard and they'll start getting on. And that's not that good you need more proactivity. What we've realised is that the reason or the way to become as successful as you can is to harness referrals. Referrals are the cheapest, quickest, best lead you can get. It hasn't changed for 20 years since I started working.

So fine-tuning that side of your business. If every business says it, and it's been said for the last 20 years that I've been listening, when you ask yourself how much money did you spend on getting introductions or referrals? Zero. How important is it to your business? Priceless. So you've got a priceless solution, but you spend zero time thinking about it and zero time planning it.

That's what you need to spend your focus on. If you can get an introduction service, and that's why we call it introduction rather than referral because everybody expects that when you refer something there has got to be some business there. It's not. I just want to meet more people. Because the more people I meet, the more business I'm going to do.

So just get me to meet more people. It's that introduction element. It's that you're asking a different question. Obviously, we've done a great job or you wouldn't still be here. But it's , "who wouldn't benefit from that?"

Everybody you know will know someone. So there will definitely be someone even if it is just one person that you introduce me to – not refer me – because I just want a chat. And suddenly you have double the people to talk to.

Early retirement is probably the focus of most people and I really start a chat about the fact that when you get to retirement 10 years early, who you going to play golf with? Probably your best buddy.

Has he got a plan to retire 10 years early or not? I don't know. Let's go find out. Okay. So give me your best buddy's number. Give him the opportunity just to say no. He's going to meet me for 20 minutes of conversation, you know how we work, we'll see how it is. See where it is. If he's got some stuff in place, brilliant. But then I know that you've got somebody to play golf with you when you want to retire early so you can really enjoy the results of all the hard work you've put in.

So then we go off and find the next best buddy. If he can't play golf that week, who are you going to phone next? Let's just carry on. Give me his number.

I think it's important to put an obligation on your client to tell people how good we are, because, ultimately, they're going to go off on a Saturday and say, oh, I'm retiring next week. And then says "what do you mean you're retiring". My mate Liam says that I can. Well, I can't afford to retire. Why not? You got the same job as me. You got the same income" "but I can't".   That's a bit unfair on your best pal, that you didn't pass on my number. He is now going to have to work another 10 years – what a rubbish friend you are!

You've got to put the obligation on them. If you believe that your service is as good as it can be and it's brilliant, who's not going to benefit from it? But you just put the question in that makes them say that nobody. Who's not going to benefit from it? He'll say, nobody. Then everybody does. If nobody's not going to benefit, then everybody does. So give me everybody you know – I've turned it from one client into lots.

I think fundamentally, that's what we're teaching those guys, our new advisers. It's difficult because they just want people that are just there waiting for them to offer business to. But it never happened for me, and it never happened for Simon, my business partner that you go out and they're just there. As I said, you don't open the door on Monday morning and people queueing up wanting a pension scheme. It doesn't happen. So you just go out and meet more people. The more you meet, the more business you get.

Paul: That's good. Last one. If you were going to give another business owner, some advice what would that advice be?

Liam: I'd always say take advice from the experts. It depends on what business you're in, but go and talk to people because they might just give you that inspirational idea or knowledge or actually take away something that you don't need. Everybody expects that I do my own accounts and stuff, but I don't because it just doesn't interest me so I pass that on and that just gives me more free time because my time is priceless. Just pass it on to people that are good at it. If there's something that you're stuck in, and you're swimming in soup, it'll be a certain job that you just don't want to do and you've put off forever and ever, is just pass it on to somebody that loves it. There are plenty of people out there that probably love doing that swimming in soup bit that you're really just hating.

Paul: You have to get your head around that. People don't do it because they're scared about the cash. They're not realising the opportunity cost. The fact that you doing this thing that you hate will take you longer. It'll stress you out. It will just suck all this time and energy.

Even at just a "maths" level, if you're at a hundred quid an hour and your bookkeeper's at 10 to 15, they'll do in two hours what'll take you four hours. Four hours of non-earning time and stress. People miss this whole concept. They don't do it. They don't give it away early enough because they think they can't afford it, but actually, they can't afford not to.

Liam: It's getting help as early as you can. It doesn't have to be employees. It could be anybody Someone outsourced. And it's just being able to trim you job done so you are doing the stuff that you are good at. It might look like you've got the biggest job in the world to do, but it all starts with the first step. So every job can be trimmed down, and you figure out the stuff that you're brilliant at, and the stuff that you know you're not going to be brilliant at, and pass that kind of stuff elsewhere. Pull in as many favors as you can. Get it done for free, if you can.

You are not your customer

You are not your customer

Value is a funny thing. What is valuable to one person is a huge waste to another and it will always be that way. For some the £1000 pound watch is a critical part of their persona for others it's a £990 waste of money.

The important thing here is that you don't make judgments about what other people will pay based on your own opinion. You are not your customer. Chances are neither are you staff, your family and friends and crucially neither are most of the other business owners you meet. Just because you wouldn't pay that much or that little for something doesn't mean no-one else will.

What ever you choose to charge – there will be someone out there who will buy it. There are 1000's of every day example to back this up.

Therefore, it is really important that as a business owner you do not try and second guess what other people perceive as valuable. There are a huge amount of often very personal factors that go into buying decisions.

People will often pay a lot more for someone they see as an expert in their field, just for peace of mind and are genuinely put off by someone who they perceive as 'too cheap' to be able to offer a good service.

This is a big one for you to understand as it is often a crucial part of what stops businesses making more money through higher prices. The notion that people "won't pay that much" is simply not the truth. People will pay for what THEY think is valuable.

Take baked beans... It's one cost for a branded can in a budget supermarket and another if you buy it from Harrods. It's the exactly the same can but people pay for the experience and kudos...and are very happy to do so.

Similarly think about socks you can buy one pair for £1 or one pair for £726, (yes really!) but they do the same job. They are made and crucially "delivered" in very different ways but they both keep your feet warm!

The universal truth here is that the customers will pay for what they think is valuable, whether it be an extra level of service, (think car washing when you have a car service) or working with someone who is the expert in their field.

As a business owner you get to choose your prices – choose wisely!

Book bonus available here:
www.marketingjumpleads.com/game-changer-book-bonuses

Look into the whites of their eyes

Look into the whites of their eyes

Whether it's an online webinar or a room full people, pulling together an event to 'tell your story' and share your expertise to many, instead of one, is a very smart business move. In today's buyer-empowered world, marketers need to seize every opportunity to start a relationship, generate goodwill and earn the trust of prospective buyers.

It's tempting to stick to marketing options with the least amount of effort and money, but a solid marketing mix which incorporate events is critical to connecting with as many potential customers as possible.

A good event perfectly positions you and your business, the audience motivates each other and you can accomplish some exciting goals - direct sales, list building, confidence for future sales, connections and an insight into what and how you can help your customers in the future. The 'liveness' of the event gives you an understanding of how best to serve your customers as you both look into the whites of each other's eyes!

If you are planning any kind of event and are naturally worried about filling the room or web-space, you are not alone. Getting butts in the seats of your workshops and seminars or a live on-line audience can be a challenge, but worth the effort.

"Events can be central to your revenue growth, or an enormous waste of time. You get to decide." - Matt Heinz, President, Heinz Marketing

Every business seeks to stand out from their competition, and event marketing can help you do just that. Whether you are hosting a small webinar, a large-scale international tradeshow, or an executive-level private function, event marketing needs to be an integral part of your marketing mix. After all, a strategic combination of online and offline marketing is essential to your company's bottom line.

Getting bums on seats (especially paying bums) is getting ever harder. Like everything there is more choice for the attendee and if we are honest the quality of many events just isn't that good.

Done well though, with proper thought, planning and follow-up, running your own event can be REALLY powerful and profitable.

When putting so much time and energy into planning your event, you want to make sure that you do the promotion right. To generate the highest amount of registrants, you need a mix of email, social, public relations, and other types of paid promotions to get the biggest bang for your buck.

By communicating with your audience early and often, leading up to the event, you will have a better turnout as your event will be top of mind for your attendees. Successful event promotion will consist of a series of touches that may include press releases, emails, direct mail, social and picking up the phone.

While today's buyers increasingly tune out commercials, avoid online advertisements, and delete promotional emails, events can get them fired up about who you are and how you can help them. With a well-planned and executed event, you can create a shared experience worth remembering.

Book bonus available here:
www.marketingjumpleads.com/game-changer-book-bonuses

Think more

Think more

This might sound like a bit of a lightweight tip but if you want a real game changer, this is it!

It's a difficult one to explain clearly because most business owners will deny it but the simple truth is that vast majority of business owners don't spend any where near enough time **thinking** about what they are doing. They have their eyes down in their business, to the extent that decisions are taken without missing a stride. They are busy in the noise of the day-to-day workings of the business and as such they very rarely take time to give the decisions that will affect their future, any consideration. It's like when you go on a car journey, sometime you can get to your destination without remembering the drive.

It's not about looking at every single decision in minute detail. It's about having a really clear picture of what is the right thing to do and when is the right time to do it.

If you look at all the big business owners and all the successful entrepreneurs, they are big thinkers. They are not doing it in a "philosopher's" kind of way but they do take time to think (and talk about it with their team) before they press ahead.

Often even a short ten minutes of time to run through various options or brainstorm with those around you can make a significant difference to the outcomes.

A lot of this comes down to time management issues but there is also a consciousness issue is well. Business owners dash around unconsciously. It's easy to get trapped in the day-to-day without taking any time to work out if what you're doing are the right things to get you where you really want to go.

If you're really serious about your business moving forward, it won't happen without thought.

So give yourself some time, block it out in your diary and let your mind run over what is going on in your business.

Get your team together to discuss new ideas or existing problems.

If you are on your own, go and find business owners who think like you and meet them regularly. Who you spend your time with will significantly affect your outcomes. Choose wisely.

You don't need to be Aristotle – but being conscious about the decisions that you take will get you closer to where you want to be.

Book bonus available here:
www.marketingjumpleads.com/game-changer-book-bonuses

Marc Wileman *SublimeScience*

Marc Wileman is best known for firing smoke rings, making slime and winning investment on Dragons' Den. He's inspired more than 500,000 children to discover how awesome science can be with the Award-Winning Sublime Science Party. His dedication to changing the way science is taught has even been recognised by Her Majesty Queen's Award for Innovation.
sublimescience.com

Discover how to guarantee your child's party is absolutely unforgettable and get your free science experiment book at: www.SublimeScience.com

Paul: So, lets start here, what is it really about for you, mate? Why this? Why running your own business as opposed to having a job?

Marc: Well, I guess it's a two-pronged thing I suppose. So, specifically, why it's Sublime Science, that's all about making science awesome for children, just that thing where I've kind of always known that science is awesome. My earliest memory of it I can recall, at least to this point in my life, is listening to George's Marvelous Medicine when I was about eight.

I'd go home and randomly experimenting with anything I could find around my parents' house and just being fascinated with science, which led me all the way up to A levels, and university, and doing a master's degree in physics, and getting a first, and being super passionate about them. But, along the way, I also got really passionate about teaching, and sharing, and explaining things, and that kind of thing. And, I guess Sublime Science is like the perfect vehicle to combine the two. So it's combining teaching, and learning, and knowledge with making science awesome. So that all kind of fits together quite nicely. In terms of why run a business, that's a bit of a weird one in that I don't really know. I always kind of thought I would.

Most people I find who run a business have got someone in their family, or friends, or whatever who also runs a business. Whereas, for me, both my parents worked for the public sector as a teacher, and my mom worked for a university. And then, when I started my business, I actually didn't know anyone who ran a business, as in I literally didn't know a single person who had run a business.

I was only 22 years old when we incorporated, and got my start with the Princess Trust, and all of that kind of stuff. But I guess it's maybe a bit of narcissism or ego, but I really believed I could do something, help a bunch of people, and add a bunch of value. But I just think it's so easy to say stuff and not do it. And I guess I just kind of wanted to go out there and kind of prove it to myself as much as anything.

Paul: Do you think you could have done what you're doing as part of someone else's company?

Marc: No. Not specifically what I do and how we've done it. I think being a business owner is a truly brilliant thing. I think we, as our own community, contribute an absolutely ridiculous amount to society and create a lot of the jobs, pay a lot of taxes, all of that good stuff. But I'm not one of those people - and some people in the little business bubble get a bit this way - where it's almost like they think that the only people that are valuable are business owners. Which is not the case. And it's not like I'm a soldier. I'm not putting on a backpack and going into enemy territory to fight terrorists to keep our country free. I'm creating products and services and selling them in a safe, democratic, first-world country.

So, I think that perspective matters. I've got friends that are humanitarian aid workers, and soldiers, and things of that nature, and those are massive contributions. And one of the things I don't like about as a business owner, I think you come under a massive amount of criticism and unhelpfulness from the government, and negative influences in the media, and all of that stuff.

Paul: And I think it's interesting because I look at what you do and, I don't think it would be possible for you to do what you do in the way you've done it in another organisation because you are so different in the most wonderfully respectful way. What you do and how you do it is very different. And I think it's hard for companies to have an employee that does that because that's not the natural bound of it. And I think to achieve what you've achieved, I think probably it could only happen with you at the helm because you see the world very differently.

Marc: Yeah, I think if you want to make a massive impact in a relatively short amount of time, as in under a decade, you're probably going to have to take full responsibility for it and do it yourself. Yeah. I think so.

Paul: Yes I think that is the way. So on that tack then, you've spoken about the numbers before. But, what does success look like to you? When you're sitting down in, I don't know, five, ten, whatever years' time, and you look back, or you see what's around you, what does that look like? How do you know you've done what you set out to do?

Marc: I think the thing is, success is an abstract concept. I think it's a moving target, which is a good and a bad thing, right? So, whenever you achieve anything, you then set another goal and go after that. So I am in that camp of people that doesn't really believe that success is some kind of destination to arrive at. But, specifically, I think specific goals are very important, at least to me. And the one thing that, I guess when you reflect on it at some point, everyone exits every business. Somewhere down the line, that always happens. So I think, when it's all said and done, for me, it's that thing that will be the measure of success has become almost our strap-line it's making science awesome for a million children. So that as long as I can say, "We made science awesome for a million children," I'd be pretty happy with that.

Paul: Yeah, that would make sense. But, by any stretch of the imagination, you are smashing it.

Marc: Technical term.

Paul: Yeah. Well, now that we're big, smart business owners, we can use these big terms. Why have you done so well, mate? And, you're a kind of self-effacing chap, and you'll probably come back and say, "Well, we've got more to do, etc." But, why do you think you have done as well as you have done?

Marc: I was actually chatting with a mate of mine the other day about this as I knew you'd ask today. And at the risk of giving a clichéd answer, that's I think, a really fascinating question and it's kind of rattled my brain slightly these past few days. I've thought about it off and on, obviously, for years. But I guess not re-thought about that for a while because obviously, I'm in the day-to-day of my life, right? None of us sits daily reflecting on success, well hopefully anyone who's not a complete narcissist egomaniac sits around thinking, "Why have I achieved so much?" I think I'd be a very strange person if I just constantly thought that of my own accord. But you asking caused me to think about it a little bit and it caused me to ask some other people because, unfortunately, I'm not entirely sure, just to give the honest answer. I'm not entirely sure.

But I guess through asking people that have known me, I actually asked my first ever employee, Mike. I'm still friends with him now, but I hired him about six and a half years ago or something. And he left a few years ago. But I think it comes down to a few things anyway. I think it's belief in possibility is thing number one that I thought about. So, actually, kind of basic, but actually believing that it's possible to go and achieve something that many people would consider to be quite a large achievement. And I think there's a lot of ego in business, typically, and there's a lot of self-aggrandisement, and a lot of narcissism. But against all, I think underneath it all when you're going to sleep at night, you're closing your eyes or whatever, in those moments, you're on your own in life to truly, in your soul, believe that you can achieve something on a massive scale with no experience, no resources, and no skillset. I think that's quite a rare trait I know that's a very rare characteristic. So I think that would be massive thing number one.

So, yeah. I guess that's what I call belief in possibility. The second thing that's kind of the opposite end of the spectrum. The more negative end of it is actually accurate thinking. I don't like the whole positive thinking thing at all. I don't like a lot of self-help stuff, to be honest, because I think a lot of it is predicated on the assumption that if you assume everything's going to be hunky-dory, it will be, which is a fairly ridiculous and untrue assumption. So, I think having belief in a massive goal, and then secondarily, having accurate thinking. So you really try and take things for what they are, not more than what they are, and not less than what they are. So, when you fail, you learn. I mean, I've obviously failed a lot at a lot of things. I do think failing your way to success is a real thing, and I think I've just had more failures than most people have done in their lifetime by the time I'm 30.

So, I certainly failed at a bunch of stuff along the way. But I think the accurate thinking to take failure for what it is, not more than what it is. So, when I fail at something, I don't necessarily look at that as, I'm a failure. I just failed. And that is a really key distinction. Failing doesn't make you a failure. It just means you're a person that's failed. And the more successful someone is, generally, the more times they've failed. And, if you learn from that experience and move forward, I think that's a massive factor.

And the other thing I came up with was, so I guess thing number three was behavioral stuff. And it really comes down to just getting stuff done consistently over time. So I think a lot of people think that, I guess, to be successful, you've got to crush it or whatever, insert ridiculous macho phrase. But I think, really, you've just got to get some good stuff done every day for a long time, which sounds fairly dull, but it's one of these things that I think is a lot easier said than done.

Paul: Yeah. Yeah, I'd absolutely buy that. So on the other side then, why do you think most business owners struggle or fail?

Marc: I guess, there's so many things. I guess I would say it's probably mandated that they do, sadly, but there is no real cure. But just, if you look at the whole Pareto 80:20 thing, there's always going to be a non-linear distribution of results. So 20% of the group are going to get 80% of the results is a fairly true analysis. Obviously, it'll be slightly different in terms of industry, and sector, and whatnot. But business owners are no different to any other group of people in anything else that you measure. So, I believe that, if you get a million business owners, it's not really going to be possible for more than about 200,000 of them to do very well just because 200,000 of them are going to get really, really good results and 800,000 of them are not. I'm not sure. There has been so many things over history that have been trying to change that sector of results. There's so many taxes, and different legislations, and government interventions, and all this stuff.

But, I think, when it comes down to it, if you consider business 80:20 one of the signs I've actually got above me in my office is, how can I add more value? It's written above my desk. So I look at that every day. When it comes to the amount of value you add, 20% of people are going to add 80% of the value. And, your bit of success, I believe, will be in direct proportion to the amount of value you deliver. So, if 20% of people deliver 80% of the value, 20% of people are going to get 80% of the "success." And I think that's just almost like a law of nature, nothing more or nothing less.

Paul: Do you think it comes back to the fact that people aren't trying to deliver value, they're trying to run a business, make money, etc., etc.? Do you think for a lot of those people that are sat in that 80% that never quite hit the mark where they want to get to, do you think it comes down to that sort of lack of purpose? There are trying to make money rather than trying to make value - if that makes sense?

Marc: Yeah, maybe. I think, in general, I do honestly believe that business owners as a group, I think we generally work very hard compared to the vast majority of humans on earth. I think that's a true thing. I think the thing about this whole thing, I certainly didn't sort of succeed out of the gate. Starting out, obviously, I got my starting help it was a £1,750 loan from the Prince's Trust that kind of got things started. And, the learning curve and growth curve going from a small loan from the Prince's Trust, and buying a laptop and a mobile phone, and running a company out of your parents' bedroom to a national company has been by far the hardest thing that I have ever done in my life by a long, long way. And, so, I think it is actually difficult, unfortunately. I think there's a lot of self-help stuff, these magic be a millionaire in ten minutes with the magic Instagram hack or whatever that are, frankly, fairly ridiculous and never really going to do anyone any good.

But I think people work hard. I guess I think it's fundamental. Put it this way, when I started off, I would've completely vastly underestimated how difficult this would be by a factor of probably about 10. That was probably partially caused by the fact I was 22, and when you're 22, and all you've done is go to university, and I got first, and I was smart, and whatever, good for me. And, so, you have a bunch of beliefs that you're amazing and whatnot. And then, when you try and do something in the big, bad, real world, and all you have is an academic background, no experience, no connections, and no money, it's like being hit with a brick wall, quite honestly. I mean, it's immensely more difficult. And, I think a lot of people probably don't acknowledge how difficult it actually is. I think things like the Facebook movie or whatever, where one minute they're chilling out drinking a beer in a dorm room, and next minute, they're in Silicon Valley, and everyone's a billionaire, and that happens within an hour ...

Paul: Is that not how it works?

Marc: Well, I guess it is. Instagram did do it in 500 days. But other than Instagram, I think they are the only one that did it that fast, ever. And, yeah, for the vast majority of people it's not like this yeah, that's fairly distant from the actual reality.

Paul: So is that the thing you'd wish you'd known when you started, that it was going to be harder? Or is there something else you look back and think, actually, I know this thing now, I didn't know it then. If I had, that would've smoothed my progress, speeded it up? Or is it just that I wish I had known how hard it would be so I would've steeled myself a bit more?

Marc: I don't know, man. I honestly don't know. I don't think I do wish I'd known how hard it would be. I don't think I would've started, to be completely honest with you.

I think if I'd known it was going to be this difficult, I probably would never have started a business. But, because of the person I was at that stage in my life at 22 years old, I'd gone to uni, I'd gone traveling, I'd earned money just getting random jobs. And I guess, at that point, I would've considered this to be impossible. But I think the single biggest thing was that's okay, right? The optimist parties a big part of it, if you learn, and grow, and develop every day, then over time, you can obviously become the person that is capable of achieving those goals. And, that gives you a really solid shot at achieving those goals.

Paul: So if you did it all again -- and in truth, it's probably a daft question because we all learn so much. But if you did it all again, would you do it differently? Would you have kind of thought, well, actually, I'd have gone to this part of my business first and grown that, which would've then led me back to this bit?

Marc: Yeah. Yeah. Yeah. I mean, 100%. I think probably everyone would, who's paying attention to their life. But I am in that camp of people that sort of becomes almost an expression of our own experiences, I mean the kind of people that thinks you learn from all your experiences. So I certainly wouldn't change anything as much as, sometimes, the difficulties, and the failings, and all of those things are fairly horrendous at the time. I guess I hate the mindset of even considering changing that stuff, which is probably why I lie to myself and say, "I wouldn't change anything" because I just like the idea of taking things for what they are, learning from them, growing from them, and sort of moving on, and looking forward, not back. I guess that's how I've just conditioned my mentality. I don't like to consider the alternative, so I just don't.

Paul: I think I agree with you. My absolute business head said, "Yeah, of course, I'd have done it differently" knowing what I know now and knowing then. But I also have loved the journey, and I know that I wouldn't be where I am now if I'd done it differently at the start. Does that kind of make any sense?

Marc: Yeah, in a sense, it's the same kind of thing. I started my business back in 2008, so I started in the biggest recession ever, with the whole sort of world falling in

Paul: Great timing!

Marc: Yeah, everyone was kind of saying the world was done. It was like hysteria and I had no idea, back then. I had no basis of comparison, right? So I'd never not run a business in 2008. But I think the big benefit of something, a huge negative like that, it just is a huge negative, and it is not really that controlled by me, I think pretty much everyone apart from a few wonderful exceptions, wonderful people in my life, but the vast majority of people said, "Don't do it. Don't start a business now when you're 22 years old, when Lehman Brothers has just gone bankrupt, and the world is melting, and you don't have any contacts, or financial security, or know what you're doing." Pretty much everyone said, "Don't do that" except for a few fairly brilliant people. But I'm really glad that I did because I think that takes away a massive amount of the fear for me in terms of I know I'll never be in a position that's that bad again because even if the economy goes worse at some point in my life than 2008, which I believe it probably will, I won't be in that environment with no skillset ever again. And, so, I think sometimes you can be so fearful of taking risks and things because your mind plays tricks on you, like all the bad stuff that could happen. But going through something terrible, from a business perspective at least, it removes a lot of that fear, helps the upside. But I've only sort of realised that this past year, weirdly, and that was like eight years ago. But with the whole talk of Brexit and stuff, a lot of people have been asking me, "Are you really worried?" and stuff. And, no, not in the slightest just because I just don't think it's likely to go anywhere near as bad as kind of 2008. And, even if it does, there's always something you can do. There's always a thing you could try, an innovation you could make. You could get better customers, get more customers, serve them better, innovate, grow. There's just always those options there. And I feel that, I guess at the end of the day, all you can do is acknowledge stuff for what it is and deal with it. I think living in fear of things is just not in my mentality. It's just not how I want to live my life.

Paul: I think lots of people are crippled by fear and I get it. We've all been in that dark place, where it just looks too hard, and the bank account is dwindling. I think it is easy just to get paralyzed by fear. Back to some of the stuff you said at the start, I think by having that actual utter belief that what I'm going to do is possible, I just need to work out how to do it.

Now I did say we're not going to go down any kind of one silver bullet-y kind of thing.... But is there a strategy, then, that has been, I suppose, the most powerful thing for your business? It's got you from that initial setup to where you are now. So, not a silver bullet, but a strategy, a plan almost?

Marc: I think, yeah, the single big thing is the one I think that nobody wants to hear, which is why I guess this is a cool platform for me to share it because having to obviously learn a bunch of stuff about marketing over the years, I understand why it's not talked about. But the single thing, I think, is consistency. I think it's the single least talked about, most effective thing in business is consistency because from a marketing standpoint, if I was a guru and I labeled myself as a consistency expert, I would obviously struggle to attract any clients because it sounds like the most boring thing in the history of the world, by far. But, when it comes down to it, so rarely does stuff work really brilliantly out of the gate. It often it's the beta version, and then it's 1.0, and then 1.1. Then, by version 2.0, you've got an absolutely killer product and a great way of taking it to market.

But maybe I'm just not all that smart, but I very rarely have done that on step one. I've really rarely deployed anything where, out the gate, everything's worked brilliantly. And, so, to get it to really work has been a consistent evolution of testing, and measuring, and improving, and developing. And, I think, yeah, the one thing would be systematic and consistent work and implementation of stuff. I think I'm in the quite fortunate position where I can actually say that because I don't have to have my magic system.

I don't have my magic seven-step formula.

Paul: So, as a parting shot then, mate, if you were going to dole out a bit of advice to the guys that they're definitely in the 20%, but they haven't quite got their stuff in a row yet, they're a little bit in that rabbits-in-the-headlights, they believe it's possible, they know they're going to do it, but they would just love someone just to put their hand on the tiller little bit and say, "Go that way," what would be that biggest bit of advice?

Marc: Again, depressing but true, some truth talk, implement ten things simultaneously, measure them, find the two that worked, and then do more of those and bin the other eight.

Paul: Lovely. Sound advice. I mean, I was hoping for some more whistles, and bells, and that sort of thing.

Marc: Well...I guess I'm a guru of sorts in that I do help a bunch of business owners out, and I do obviously make science awesome for a lot of kids. But I don't really feel that I have to have that signature system, the whatever you're going to call it. I don't know if you could make, "Do ten things simultaneously, test them, figure out which one's work, do more of that, and can the other ones." I just don't know if you can make that sound cool.

Paul: Yeah, but I think this is the beauty of it, I think it shouldn't sound cool. I think one of the problems with what's happened with our other business people, and, again, in the bubble that you and I inhabit there are so many goorus, with a double-o, and it's useful to some level, but it's also just too much noise. It's a little bit like losing weight and getting fit. If you want to lose weight, eat better, do more exercise. It's kind of that simple. We can dress it up. There are all kind of different things you could eat, there are different kind of exercises. But the truth is that, and I think it's the same with business - do stuff, see what stuff works, do more of said stuff.

Marc: Yeah. I mean, I think that analogy that actually you just made, is cool. I've used that a little bit before with business and nutrition. But, right now, we probably have more diets, and exercise programs, and things, right? There's more, "How to get shredded in seven minutes guaranteed," products on the planet earth right now than ever before in all of human history. But, then, we also have the biggest obesity crisis in all of human history. And I think it's pretty interesting how correlated those two things are.

Paul: I'd never thought about that, but that's interesting, isn't it?

Marc: There's a guy who wrote a book called The Twinkie Diet. Do you know what a Twinkie is? It's a sweet, American little sweet in a little wrappy.

There's a guy who only had Twinkies for like 3 months - it's like saying, "I only ate Cadbury's Crème Eggs for like 90 days," or something. And it's, obviously, the inherently most ridiculous idea in the history of mankind really.

Paul: That's amazing.

Marc: But I think, almost, that's the downside. I guess the upside of marketing is, obviously, marketing is the ability to communicate your products and services to your customers. I guess that's kind of what marketing is, I suppose, in a way. That's obviously an amazing thing because, if you can't communicate what you do to people, you're always going to be in a spot of bother. But on the opposite side of it, my Facebook feed is full of people with the magic Instagram hacks, and it's all about SnapChat. If I'm not on Blab and Periscope, and SnapChat, and Meerkat, whatever, if I'm not on all of those simultaneously, live-casting 36 times a minute, I'm going to die or something. And, obviously, that's not really true. Like you said before, that's actually, really, really unhelpful. That might be a hook to sort of tie it all in with, I suppose, because I come from a science background, right? I've got a first class degree and a master's degree in physics. And I really like science. I love it. I believe massively in the scientific method and in reasoning. And, if you look at all the amazing stuff scientists have done, like diseases cured, and life expectancy risen, and quality of life improved, and all of those things, I think it's beyond incredible.

Starting off in business, that was a massive hindrance to me because you know all this technical stuff. But that, in a lot of ways, can just lead to overwhelm and almost get in the way of just developing an awesome product and telling people about it. But as stuff has moved forward for me. The landscape's got more confusing and all of these things. I think that by applying the scientific method to business is the perfect way of kind of separating the nonsense from reality.

Does that kind of make sense? I don't really have opinions on Facebook, or SnapChat, or whatever. I just don't really, you hear people say they're a SnapChat marketer or something. And it's just funny to me because that's just a ridiculous statement. That's like me saying, "I'm pro-gravity" or "I'm pro-friction." What are you even saying? Those things kind of are what they are. But using an evidence-based approach, I think is an incredibly sensible thing to do. And, again, it's something that's not really talked about because it doesn't sound very cool.

Paul: It is an odd time that we're in. And, particularly in our business bubble, in our Marketing bubble, and the stuff that is around us.

But I think it makes it exciting if you are the sort of person that can comb through the noise and find the good bits, I think it's a fantastic time to own a business. I think if you're the sort of person that can't, I think it's an incredibly frustrating time to own a business, because there are too many gooroos telling you that this new thing is the answer to all your problems. I'm not casting aspersions here. That stuff can be really useful in the right hands. But in the wrong hands, it just creates a massive fog, and I think it slows people down.

Marc: Yeah, to leave on a positive, I guess, I think the single thing with all the negativity in the world, I guess, from the whole Brexit thing and people are having opinions on that, and obviously the prime minister resigning, and whatever, all these bits and bobs going on in the background, I think it's very easy to lose sight of we are living in the most abundant time in the history of earth. This is the most abundant moment in the history of the universe. And, if you live in a first-world democratic country even more so. I do some stuff helping out for a charity with East African playgrounds. I'm on the board of trustees there and have visited Uganda. If you look at their situation and compare it to, say, living in Central London, for example, that's a very different experience it's almost like a different world.

And, in all the nonsense, and stock market fluctuations, and prime minister resigns, or this is a vote of no confidence in this dude, or whatever, it's kind of easy to lose sight of the fact that just, logically, this is the most abundant time ever. We've got more tools and technology at our disposal than ever before. Most of them, you can rent now. So you can just rent a server. You can test Facebook out for a pound or whatever. So you can start off small, and you can test things for cheap. All the barriers to entry in business have been completely erased with the advent of technology. And, I guess it's just pure genetic fluke or whatever that I ended up being born here at this time in the world. And, yeah, I guess just having a bit of gratitude for that and recognising that this time is all we've got anyway, right?

It's all well and good, people saying, "When this economy picks up, then I'm going to do something." What if the economy never picks up? Who knows? I obviously think it will. But, you know what I mean? That's just an uncontrollable, isn't it?

Paul: And, when it does pick up, it'll unpick up again. That's just the nature of it.

Marc: Yeah, it's going to go up and down, there's going to be more competition, there's going to be less competition in some cycles, there's going to be this, there's going to be that. But, yeah, I think that's the message I'd like to leave my little thing on, if that's possible anyways, just to sort of say in that background of all the more negative media stuff that's knocking about, I just think so many people seem to have lost sight of the fact that it's right now, you live in England. I'll never have to bribe anyone to run my business here. I'm allowed to just incorporate a business and sell products and services. I don't have to pay money to stop anyone killing me or whatever. There's loads of countries in the world where that's just not true.

And there's loads of countries where they just steal your money, or you're not allowed to run a business, or there is no internet, or there are no people with money and iPhones to reach.

What we do have is absolutely phenomenal. And I guess it's easy to overlook that in, I guess, the myriad of just media scaremongering and nonsense really.

You've got to stay in control of the conversation

You've got to stay in control of the conversation

As a business owner you need to be in control of your "selling conversation" at all times. As soon as you relinquish that control back to the customer the less likely they are to buy from you and the more likely your competitors can sweep them up, never to return. As a wise man once said;

"It's not your customers or prospects job to remember to do business with you – It's your job to remind them".

If you are just waiting for your customers to remember that they might need or like what you do you are playing roulette with your future.

You have to look at it like this. Why would you leave your business' financial future in the hands of someone who has no interest in its success?

While that sounds dramatic that is exactly what most business owners are doing every day. They open up their doors or turn on their email hoping that past clients will remember to buy again or new clients will just decide to seek them out.

However, if you are in control and you nudge, and remind and give value first and send the odd offer out you have a much stronger chance of money coming in.

Let me give you an example.

I like nice clothes and I buy my brand of shirts from one particular shop. They know me, they know my name, and they know what I buy. They have a shop full of stuff which I am pretty likely to spend some money on.

But I NEVER hear from them. They are waiting for me to wake up one day and think – I quite fancy a new shirt. Which means I have all the control over our relationship and their ability to make money from me.

It would be so simple for them to take back control, something as easy as asking for my email address would be a great start. They could then drop me a line from time to time maybe with the odd offer here and there just to remind me that they are the stockist I go to for my favourite shirts.

"Hey we've some more of those shirts you like coming in next week and wondered if you fancied coming down to have a look?"

"Hey you know that great shirt you bought last week, we have found the perfect jacket to go with it."

"Hey, we've not seen you for ages and we've got some great new stock – fancy coming for a look? And I tell you what as you are one of our favourite customers here's a 20% off voucher that's valid until the end of the month."

It's so simple but so important – don't gamble your success on your prospects ability to remember you are there.

Take people's details so you can be in control of the conversation.

Book bonus available here:
www.marketingjumpleads.com/game-changer-book-bonuses

Be careful who you listen to

Be careful who you listen to

Never underestimate the power of stupid people in large groups...

The fact that you are reading this means that you are different. The only way you would have got your hands on this book is by buying, downloading an e-copy or twisting one of our arms for a free copy!! – Which by definition means you have had to go out of your way and part with some money, effort or time to get hold of it – and that activity in business owners is surprisingly rare.

Most business owners talk a great game but very rarely take action.

Now, that's great for you, but it also gives you a real problem. Because the reality is that the overwhelming majority of the people around you don't think like you which makes them look at what your doing and either think you are nuts spending actual money on growing your business or, more likely, they just don't "get it" and as such they can be, at best, no help to you. At worst they'll try to convince you you're wasting your time and they'll drag you down to their level.

They are happy just getting by covering costs, paying the tax man and settling for a short holiday each year. – Nothing wrong with that for them, but for you, as someone who is serious about their business changing – it is a big issue.

So why is it a problem?

Because as a business owner it is really difficulty to do it alone – it's a lonely and isolating place and one of the most powerful things you can do is spend time with other business owners – but if those people don't think like you, then it curbs your drive.

It's a bit like playing golf. If you play with someone worse than you then you tend to play badly but if you play with the pro you raise your game.

The facts of the matter are, it is far easier to find and spend time with people who don't want what we want – the standard networking crowd is littered with people that turn up week in week out but never move their business forward. You try and talk to them about what you are doing and topics like how much you will spend to get a customer and they look at you like you are crazy. In the absence of another voice it's easy to believe them.

However, surround yourself with the RIGHT people, people who get it – people that want to change their stars and are willing to do something about it and it changes everything! You feel that buzz, you get to talk seriously about your ideas, plans, thoughts and challenges and get useful feedback and ideas from people that are out there doing it too.

The reality of the situation is that you are 'level 4 different'...

Most people can't run a business. Most of those that do, are just trying to get by – they effectively still have a job. Some of those dream big but take no action. But some – like you, talk the talk and walk the walk.

So who you hang around with matters A LOT. For many business owners (although for most they are entirely unaware of the fact) it is the deciding factor in their success but they never try and control it.

Be clear and thoughtful on who you listen to and who's advice you take. Most importantly actively seek out opportunities to spend time with other business owners who want what you want and are out there learning and doing it.

Book bonus available here:
www.marketingjumpleads.com/game-changer-book-bonuses

Martin Norbury *Myadvocatementor*

Martin Norbury, author of #1 Amazon Bestseller I don't work Fridays, went from small-time entrepreneur to SME business owner and onto Senior Executive in a multi-million pound corporation in just ten years. Setting up his first business in 1991, using a little bit of office space lent to him by some friends, he went on to successfully exit; years later he generated unbelievable results as CEO at a multinational corporation, turning a loss of £250k per month to celebrating its first £1 of profit in just a matter of months.

Back running his own company Advocate Business Services, Martin now helps business owners who are stuck in, or stuck on, their business sack themselves through making their business more valuable, more fun and highly saleable. His ultimate goal is to help business owners choose what they do with their tomorrow through the application of his SCALE Model which is used across 50+ industries, earning him the badge of The Scalability Coach.
A business turnaround specialist, Martin is actively involved in buying and selling SMEs, and advises companies on their exit strategies, how to leverage deals and maximise shareholder value.

As well as providing Non-Executive Director support for SMEs, Martin helps global giants focus on their business improvement through people development and effective personal management.

Martin has won a multitude of awards, including: Business Mentor of the Year 2015, Britain's Top 50 Business Adviser 2014, National Entrepreneur of the Month June 2013, and Business Growth Advisor of the Year 2012.

Martin is an approved Myers-Briggs Type Indicator® Qualified Practitioner, Fellow of the Institute of Coaching, and Fellow of the Chartered Management Institute.

As well as helping more entrepreneurs achieve success, Martin will be donating proceeds from book sales to a charity close to his heart, Sands, who support those affected by the death of a baby, and promote research to reduce the loss of babies' lives.

Martin doesn't work Fridays!

http://myadvocatementor.com/

Paul: We'll start with this one, so for you Martin, what is it really about? Why do you do it, as opposed to having a job, let's say?

Martin: Oh, that's interesting. Okay. So I do what I do I suppose, primarily because I had a bit of a life-changing event in 2010. And that life-changing event, where I lost my daughter, meant that I wanted to change what I was doing. I was originally working in corporate life as a CEO in a large company and decided that that wasn't what I wanted to do anymore because I wanted to spend more time with my family. And, actually, that was a really important part. And then 18 months later, we had twins and that made me really refresh everything I did. That's actually why we're doing what we're doing anyway because, if I'm spending all the time at work and doing nothing else, then that's going to be not great for the family, not what I want to do. So I made a conscious decision to take off Fridays, which I have done ever since. And, so, I don't work Fridays. I work generally from around about ten o'clock until four o'clock. I do a little bit before, a little bit after, but then most of the time's with the family. So, once we discovered that, we realised that what we do as a business is we help other business owners choose what they do with their tomorrow. And we do that by helping the businesses scale their business and then exit through either selling it or spending more time doing what they want and getting other people to run their business. So that's why we do what we do.

Paul: So leading on from that then, what does success look like for you?

Martin: Well, success always changes the goalpost. I think that's one thing I realised. So my first success was just to not work Fridays and still carry on doing other things. And I did that, but then I started creeping into working Saturdays. It's like, I don't work Fridays, but I work Saturdays, Sundays, and late Mondays, and stuff like that. So success was actually to really focus on that and not do that, which I did. My children go to school this September and part of success was choosing the school that we wanted them to go to, whether that was a state-run school or a private school, it didn't matter. So we drew up a list of what we wanted, we went to ten different schools. As it ended up, it was a private school, but that was purely because of what we wanted for the children. And on those lines, that was success.

Success also means spending time with them outside of the UK, somewhere hot. I would say summer's my favourite season of the year, and we don't get a lot of summer in the UK, so I want a place. So it's having a place in the sun. So that's something we decided we wanted to do a few years back. We sat down and mapped out what we wanted to do and we take possession of our new place in the sun in October. And that's great because the kids will grow up with a place they can consider home somewhere else, but also we can use as projects as well. So we can go out there during the summer holidays and do stuff, which is the third part really of the success formula for us is, there's no point in having a business where I have to work in it constantly and have to be a part of it. So whilst our business now is largely around myself, we've now got a formula where we're growing the business, but through other people using our methodology and our formula. And that kicks off in September as well. So the first consultant employee, who will be another CEO type person, comes in. We use our scale model, they'll go out and they'll do that, which means then we are not tied to the business. So children will be in a good school, we'll have a nice place to go when it's hot -- when it's cold here and hot over there, and we'll have a business, not a hobby or not a lifestyle business.

Paul: I'm not sure this is a useful question, but to hear what you have achieved is really inspiring, why do you think you've done so well?

Martin: I do get asked that question a lot, as in, is there a gene or is there something in somebody that, when they put their mind or do something, they get the right results? And I don't believe it is because I've met lots of very different people who are successful. So I think there's a few things that I would say. One is having, I suppose, the determination not to let anything stop you. I was at a recent event run by a guy called Anthony Robbins, a phenomenal success. He's done lots of things. But, out of the whole five days spent with him and his organisation, one thing he said which really resonated with me is the "tyranny of the how". I've never heard that before and I realised it's just a more eloquent way of putting what I would always put, which is I don't let anything stop me. I don't let a "how" stop me..

I want to earn this much money. I make that my mission to find a way of doing it and not go, "Oh, but how do I do that?" because there's always a way of doing it. The world's got lots of opportunities out there. So it's just finding the way to do it and not say, "Oh, how do I do that?" because, as soon as you say that, you stop yourself. To me it's, "Okay, we need to get people into our business to run business. So let's just starting finding them." You don't say, "How?" About ten years ago one, of my colleagues in a company I used to run said we should double our commission fee to our network, basically, which would, of course, double our revenue. And all of my leadership team just went into this big meltdown of how. And I just went, "Yeah, let's do that." And it was like, "Okay." And they said, "Well..." And I said, "Well, let's just look at all the things that we can do once we've done that. So let's go fast-forward into that point, and then we'll work out how afterwards. But let's not stop us at the first gate when there's lots of other gates that we can go through. Let's make sure that we understand what we're aiming for." So I suppose, in essence, it's just having that view of where you want to get to and just not letting "how" stop you.

Paul: So on the other side of that, why do you think most business owners struggle or fail?

Martin: I think this will be quite controversial, but I think they do not know enough about running a business, and then they don't care that they need to know enough about running a business. As in, there's lots of things you need to do, like you need to understand your sales, your marketing, your numbers, all these things. And too many people think there's a magic bullet or the secret thing out there to do it. And we both know, we spent a lot of time with people that are very successful at doing certain things in business, but there is no magic bullet. There is no secret formula. The key to it is to do the basic stuff over and over again. Get good at it, learn it, understand it, know your business, keep going and going and going. So one of the major things -- I'll say this is a little bit controversial. I just think too many people think it will be easy, are a bit lazy, don't do the right work, and expect things to happen. And, when it doesn't, they give up.

95% of businesses fail in ten years and it's not because they don't produce great products. I've seen wonderful, wonderful businesses that failed, producing great services and great products, and it's just because they don't care enough to do something about it. Unless they care enough -- they do care, but not enough to do something about it. So they just end up not doing it, or going back to a job, or something else. And I think that's just a criminal thing. I've spent lots of time with mastermind groups where people go, "Yeah, I'm going to do that, I'm going to do that, I'm going to do that." They come back next time, they've not done it, but they expect a different result. Absolutely crazy.

Paul: Frustrating, isn't it?

Martin: Oh, massively.

Paul: So, looking back now, is there one thing you wish you'd known? Not really a silver bullet, but is there like a, "Ah, I wish I had... now I know that, I wish I had done that when I was, you know, 10, 15, 20 years ago sort of thing?"

Martin: Lots of people might say, based on the measures of other people's success, that I'm doing okay, but for me, I'm probably still underachieving because I'm a little bit lazy. But I sort of focus in the right things. I focus the 80/20 rule quite a bit. I make sure that the 20% that really gets the 80% results is where I focus on. That's what I've always tended to do. But the biggest lesson I've seen and in the masterminds I've run with you Paul, as well, is the activity.

Paul: Yeah. Always.

Martin: People just don't do enough. They talk to me and say, "Oh, yeah, we haven't had lots of sales in the last month." I say, "Well, how many prospects or customers have you spoken to and what have you said to them?" It's real basic stuff, isn't it? If you haven't spoken to enough people about what you do, you're never going to achieve the results. So, for me, it's activity. It's doing -- just getting out there and doing stuff. You do enough of it, one is, you learn, the market gets to hear what you're doing. You're road-testing your product and service. You're improving it if you listen enough. It gets better and better. People start buying it; people start wanting it; people start referring it. But, if you sit there and plan and prepare and do all these wonderful things that you should do, which means not doing the right things, just doing things right I suppose, then you'll never get anywhere.

Paul: If you could do it all over again, is there anything you'd do differently?

Martin: Maybe take a bit more of a leap of faith with the right team. I've looked at businesses that have been successful that I've run or been involved in, and it always comes down to the right team really. So starting a business, the ones that start and accelerate their business are the ones that put into place quite quickly the right three key roles: the right sales team, the right financial team, and the right delivery team. And what happens basically with entrepreneurs is they look at their cash. They go, "Oh, if I pay someone to do that, then it's not in my pocket, so I won't do it." But, if you pay good money for really good sales, really good operations, really good finance, that's three roles, not only are you getting the best -- better than you because you might not know those things, but you're also getting another 200 hours a week, nearly, at the early stages. Of course, 200 hours a week is a lot more than 30 or 40 or 50 hours a week, which means you're accelerating your growth as well. And I don't think enough entrepreneurs realise that. I'm involved in probably three or four other businesses apart from my own. And I've not entered one of them as an acquisition or as a buy-in without a team, so let alone the original team that's a part of the business, but also bringing in key players for me as well.

Paul: So beyond having the right people in place, what do you think has been the most potent strategy, if that's the right word, for your business?

Martin: It's what I refer to in my book as it was hidden in plain sight. It's always been hidden in plain sight for me, and I only realised it as I was sort of finishing the book. The last chapter says there's something about what I've done that's been really successful. It's in the book, but it's not explicit. And this is it, really, in some way. It's being known wide as you can by the right people for doing what you do. So basically, it's doing your own personal PR. And that's one thing I've been quite good at doing, is aligning myself with people that have got a bigger message than I have. So My book was foreworded by Daniel Priestley, and most people have heard of Daniel Priestley. He's quite a well-known figure in the entrepreneurs' world and in, well, actually UK, America, Australia. But that meant that a lot of people read the book because he was attached to it, which meant we got quite a bit of business from that as well. I'm not saying we did that specifically. I was working with Daniel anyway, and it made a natural thing.

But all I do is I try and get other people to tell the right people about what we do. And by doing that, that means that we get our name wider, wider, and wider. Too many businesses are very, very local, as in it's basically their customers are in their shouting distance. So they shout in their local area through networking and stuff like that. That's where they get their business. But, most of all, that's about survival mode. If you can do that but get across the next county or the next territory or the next country or wherever, then suddenly, you've got an actual business. And I think that's been probably one of the secret formulas that we've had or something that we've done, is we've been very, very good at making sure the right people hear our message.

Paul: So, on that then, if you were to give a bit of advice to an ordinary business owner, they've got the dreams, they've got the drive, but they just want to almost hear it from someone else, what would be the biggest bit of advice you could give them?

Martin: Yeah. Okay. So, apart from what I've said, because you do need to know those sorts of things, is actually just having some understanding of what's the most important thing they need to do next because too many people spend their time focused on doing immaterial stuff. I've got a client we both know well, so I won't mention them. He's very, very focused on goals, and doing stuff. And I spoke to him the other day, I said, "You're still not getting the right results because, if you do the right things, it manifests itself into the right results." So I said, "Well, just what have you been doing the last couple of days And they're really, really pleased about telling me what they've been doing. And at the end of the call I just said, "Look, X, you're pissing around with your business. You're doing all the detail, the nitty-gritty, all the getting the contracts drawn up, getting the webpage looking great, all that sort of stuff; whereas, someone with more determination could have been out there talking to ten customers by now about what they do, what they could do, doing the right thing and getting the right results." And that's the difference, I think, with the business owners that I've met that do really, really well, is they just focus on what the next thing is that's the most important thing in their business and don't try and get caught up in the noise, and the detail, and all this sort of stuff because no one really cares. I've sold products, and you've done the same, without even having a product to sell.

But I've got a customer to buy. And that's just so much more important. And, obviously, I would never sell something unless I intended to deliver it. But one of the best marketing forms out there is start by getting the product "description" out there.   "Now, I'm starting a new, say, coaching program." It's a program that lasts a year. It's every 10 days. It's 30 minutes. You get all our products. And I put a big thing out there and I get 30 people saying, "That sounds great." And I say, "Well, all I need is a thousand-pound deposit and off we run." Now, I could get thirty grand in my business like that and I haven't even got a product yet.

But, now, I've got a product because I've got 30 people that want it. So what's the most important thing for me to do now? So once I've got the customers is now design the product. I can now design it because I've got my customers. Lots of people design it with no customers. So one is, they don't even know what the product should be doing because nobody's told them about it, and two is they spend all their time designing and it's something that nobody wants. Bizarre, really bizarre.

Be clear why you are selling

Be clear why you are selling

Most business owners are getting a customer to make a sale...

The really smart ones are making a sale to get a customer.

Think about the lifetime value of a customer. Even if you think your product is a one off (it isn't) there is a real value in having a customer;

You know them
You know what they buy
They trust you enough to buy from you
You are in a better position then anyone else to sell to them again, whether that is for your product or someone else's.

It is a truth that in business today the overwhelming majority of business owners, (and quite often the sales people in those businesses) don't think any further than that first sale.

Another way of saying this is that ordinary business owners think in terms of growing sales while the really smart business owners thinking in terms of growing the amount of customers.

It might sounds like semantics but there is a big difference in both activities and results.

The point is that smart business owners see their customers as an important asset with an ongoing and expandable value. As such they will go above and beyond what their competitors will do to bring a customer to them in the first place, both in terms of cost and value. For them a customer is not just a route to the cash via that first transaction – quite the opposite.

You will often hear people talk about buying a customer, and they are not talking about purchasing a load of data. They are talking about the spend they are prepared to make to secure that initial transaction. Because they know once they have a customer they can build a relationship and keep making sales to them.

Do this you need to understand the lifetime value of your customer. How much will they spend with you in the first 90 day, 1 year, 3 years...

Don't kid yourself that people will only buy once, there are very few businesses that are genuinely only single transaction (and most that think they are - aren't). There will always be an opportunity to make money out of a strong relationship – even if it's just as an affiliate.

Thinking about 'buying' customers simply makes your marketing better. What is more likely to make you want to buy a carpet? An email telling you how great the carpets are, or a nice presentation box landing on your doormat with some samples in?

The great news is that most of your competitors are trying to get customers for the cheapest possible price. They don't understand this concept so don't spend anything acquiring customers and as such just disappear into the noise. The good news is you don't really have to spend much more to stand out.

So ask yourself this? How much is a customer worth over the lifetime of their relationship with me and so how much would I pay to attract them to me away from my competitors.

Because the reality is the more you spend to get them, the more likely they are to choose you in the first place AND the longer they are likely to stay with you. This opens up more opportunities to sell more to them.

Break Even on the Front End, Break the Bank on the Back End

 Book bonus available here:
www.marketingjumpleads.com/game-changer-book-bonuses

Create a shopping list

Create a shopping list

We have spoken about it elsewhere in the book, and it will always be a recurring theme but one of the key things that differentiate the really successful business owners and the rest is the way they think. That goes for their attitude towards their earnings too.

The reality is most business owners define their lifestyle by what is left at the end of the month. They work hard, pay the bills then decide what they can do with what is left. However, if you look at the really successful business owners, they choose a lifestyle and then find a way to make it happen.

They buy the cars, wear the clothes and book the holidays first because then they have to find a way pay for it.

Now to be very clear here, we are absolutely not advocating racking up a huge debt or heading out on a wild spending spree, but booking that family holiday, that needs to be paid for by a certain date will really help focus your mind.

It makes it more 'real' and makes failure to achieve the goal that bit more 'painful' and thus makes you that bit more likely to do what needs to be done to make sure you don't feel that pain.

It's like having pictures of what you want to achieve over your desk, but with a timescale attached

It is a bit more of a 'high risk' strategy and will work best in conjunction with everything else but we know a lot of business owners that use this strategy to 'force' themselves onwards. The interesting thing is that the overwhelming majority of the time – they make it happen, as one of our Marketing JumpLeads Members put it,

"It was a big step for me and very scary, but I had been promising the family 'a holiday to remember' for years and had never quite delivered. So I just booked it, knowing that I had 6 months to pay the balance. And it changed everything, there was no way I would go back to them and say we couldn't actually go.

It changed what I did day to day. I stopped procrastinating and just got more of the right stuff activities done – and I paid the balance off a month earlier than I planned! We had an amazing time on holiday and it felt brilliant that I had set out to do it and achieved it. I booked a better hotel already for next year!"

Put yourself under some pressure – make it real

Reputation is everything

Reputation is everything

The term 'Public Relations' makes PR sound very serious and very formal and primarily about writing press releases and courting journalists.

When in fact almost all communications, social updates and even meetings form part of your business PR - **how you manage your reputation.** What do you say about yourself and what do others say about you and your business?

PR infiltrates everything you do if you want to build a strong business and make quality connections, have strong personal relationships and solid friendships.

> " If I was down to the last dollar of my marketing budget I'd spend it on PR!" Bill Gates

Avoiding boasting, a good PR strategy builds and influences peoples opinions of you and your business – this of course includes journalists, but also ALL your target audiences who have an effect on you and the success of your business – and your life!

PR is a powerful way to get your target audience to know, like and trust you – but you are not advertising yourself and or blowing your own trumpet. **You are getting someone else, of influence, to do it for you – a third party endorsement that improves your profile and protects your reputation.**

In our digital, social world where nothing is sacred or beyond interrogation, managing your personal and business reputation is harder than ever. Yet we have new and exciting opportunities and channels to harness opinion and build a reputation far and wide, like never before in history.

'Media' is no longer the printed word alone. In fact social platforms such as Twitter have allowed you to become a kind of citizen journalist where you can approach your target media directly with your comments and material.

If you can raise your profile above those of your competitors, new customers will easily find you, understand what you do and offer and how you are different from their current supplier or others in your niche.

In this way, PR is not just for the 'bigger' businesses. It's for every size of business and in every sector. Good PR is a fantastic way to build and grow your business and it should just become part of your business DNA, 'your way of thinking and working'. With some practice it can be ingrained in your marketing mix and rather than it being 'something else on the list', it's simply how you treat and communicate your message, to encourage others to spread the word about you and your business.

Public Relations is more exciting than ever, but also more challenging. A bad printed article buried in a newspaper could easily have gone unnoticed by the majority of people who matter to your business. But this the head in the sand approach today, with us all under intense constant scrutiny, simply just won't work.

Harnness this incredible opportunity. Take control of your reputation and consistently work at encouraging others to share your expertise and stories.

"It takes 20 years to build a reputation and five minutes to ruin it. If you think about that you'll do things differently" Warren Buffet

Book bonus available here:
www.marketingjumpleads.com/game-changer-book-bonuses

Oli Luke *oliluke.com*

Oli Luke is a client acquisition specialist that works with experts/coaches/consultants to help them win more of their ideal clients and grow their profits.
www.oliluke.com

Paul: So as our starting point, then, what's it really about for you? Why are you doing this? Why are you doing this as opposed to working for someone else?

Oli: Good question. So I suppose it's two reasons. Firstly, I think running a business is really good fun. You get to help people. It gives you opportunities to achieve things that you wouldn't achieve if you had a job. I suppose the big overall thing is control. You've got control of your time. You've got control of how much money you can make, which then gives you control to go to places that you want, travel when you want, take your family where you want.

So I suppose the huge big part is control. And, secondly, I suppose it kind of comes under control again, it gives you time to spend with the family, to support the family, and you can take control of your own time and money, which is the Holy Grail for me, whereas in a job you've got no control of either. So that's the big reason I run a business. It's good for managing your time, you've got control of your life.

Paul: So moving on from that now, what does success look like for you? How do you know that what you're doing is delivering what you want it to do? How are you measuring that?

Oli: Good question. So how do I define success? Start there. So the bit that's always stuck with me was when I read The 4-Hour Work Week by Tim Ferriss. And he had the concept of the new rich, where he says, the old rich are the people who have millions in the bank, but work crazy hours, and burn all their relationships with their family because of work and everything like that, whereas the new rich is more focused on time, and that's really resonated with me.

For example, it could be a business that makes £30,000 a month, but they've got to work 50 hours a week at 200 hours a month. Quick maths, that's... £150 an hour value. Or it could be the business that makes £10,000 a month and only works 10 hours a week and 40 hours overall, which then makes £250 an hour. I'd say that's good maths.

I think time's the big issue. So in my mind, I've made it when I've got complete control of my time, when it's the choice to work. So at the moment, I wouldn't say I've got the choice to work when I want, although I've got control. If I were to take two weeks off now, it'd cause a little bit of friction. I see success as when you can completely pick your hours. If you don't want to work, you don't want to work. If you want to work, you want to work. That's how I define success.

Paul: We know things are good and you're doing really well. Why do you think that is?

Oli: Thanks, firstly. It's very nice of you of you to say that.

I suppose the big thing is not settling, always striving to get it better or charge more money in order to work with better people or have a better business. So just to make sure everything's moving in the right direction all the time. I think, personally, I'm very aware of how fast time ticks, and I live in fear of letting time pass me by. To get really personal, I live in fear of having unfulfilled potential. That really scares the life out of me.

I think at many points I could have settled for what I have and could have reduced my hours, and, I suppose, got closer to what I define as success. But I'm very scared of 15, 20 years passing, and I look back, and I realise how much potential there was to do really cool things, and it was unfulfiled. I suppose that's the big driver. I suppose, when I look back at that, that's what's got me to this point, and what will get me further up.

Paul: So on the converse of that, then, why do you think most business owners struggle and often, ultimately, fail achieving what they want?

Oli: I suppose it's a flip of that, i.e., they're stuck in their ways. They're not willing to invest, learn, take risks, try something new. They tend to copy the rest of the market and not want to step out of line. I think 99% of business owners are in this way of copying everyone else, not wanting to do anything too different, thinking the only way to grow a business is organically. They only grow a business when referrals come in or over time, when, really, marketing is essential, good marketing is like having cheat codes for your Play Station. You can generate customers easy. You can increase your fees. You can find new avenues to make more money. I think once you get to grips with marketing, it allows you to grow much quicker. But I think most business owners fear marketing. They rely on organic growth, and they're not willing to try something new or invest or learn.

Paul: What do you wish you'd known when you started because, obviously, I've known you for a while, and I've seen where you've come from. We used to work together. When that first day, you shut the front door, and you realised, sh*t, I'm a business owner. Looking back now, is there one thing that you thought, I wish I'd done that, I wish I'd started that sooner?

Oli: The big thing to me is I started at the bottom and worked my way up so I used to charge hardly anything, and then over time, I've just increased my fees, and grown my knowledge, and everything along them lines. If I could go back now, I think the one thing I wish I knew was the power of price elasticity.

So all I would have done is I would have niched down really well, found a really hungry market, positioned myself well to that market, and then got them good results, and that would have allowed me to charge what I want. Probably on a very exclusive basis.

Either that, or worked on a results basis for a very hungry market. I went down the route of work with anyone and charged very low prices. Anyone with a credit card and a pulse could be a client. Then, over time, I've learned the power of having the right clients, finding your niche, who you can help, and who you can get the best results for. Once you find that, it allows you to charge what you want. I wish it was the other way around, and I knew that from day one because I would have saved many hours of ball ache.

Paul: I think that we've all done that kind of picking of clients. I think so much of it is confidence based. I think if you could distill confidence and put it as a drug, as it were, and give yourself a shot of that day one just to back yourself, I think you'd all be further forward. We get a lot of brand new guys coming to us saying, "Look, can you help us?" and a big part of it is getting them to back themselves. Particularly on price. I think price is so much in the business owner's head, way more than it is in the prospect's, or the client's head.

Oli: Exactly.

Paul: But it's a difficult thing. If you start by thinking, well, why is someone going to pay me 250 quid an hour? Then they probably won't

Oli: Exactly.

Paul: So if you did it all over again, is that the thing? You'd have just charged more earlier kind of thing?

Oli: Exactly. Yeah, to find a hungry market and provide an exclusive, premium price solution, and it would have been as simple as that. Like I said, confidence is the big one. You do start at the bottom, especially if you come out of a full-time job because to, all of a sudden, make the leap from earning £1500 to £2000 a month, to think you can, all of a sudden, demand that from one client for a few hours of your time or a couple of days, there's a massive mental shift that needs to happen. So, yeah, it does take time, but once you actually start to develop confidence from day one, then, yeah, that's definitely what would have happened.

Paul: We don't do silver bullets here, but is there one strategy that has driven the biggest results?

Oli: Yeah, I suppose so. So it's finding the most effective way of winning customers, then finding a way of consistently and predictably getting them into a position to buy. So what I mean by this is if I go back, when I first started, the customer journey of how people can give me money was so all over the show.

What was the real turning point was when I worked out, what's the best way I can sell this service I offer? And it quickly works out that it was over the phone. And then I thought, "Okay, how can I get people to speak to me on the phone?" Let's turn it into a strategy session so I give them value. Perfect. How can I get people into a strategy session? Let's pitch at the end of a webinar or pitch the end of some training. How can I get people into that webinar and training? Then I need to get someone to an invitation or a registration page. How do I get them to that? And then it all comes back to traffic. I think finding the end goal and working out how you best sell to people, and then working it backwards, that was a big turning point. It made it very simple. It works out that the main funnel that I needed in my business.

Paul: What about non-business stuff, mates? The stuff, peripherals. Not the actual activity in your business. What else do you think has been instrumental? I know for me one of the big things from day one is that when I first started in business, I hung around with the wrong people. I sort of went networking without even thinking about it, and I've said it before, but it was so dull and uninspiring that it sucked energy rather than gave energy. Is there something other than your actual marketing strategy that's worked?

Oli: I suppose that the biggest turning point was the mental shift that I made from the time where I thought all I deserved was low fees and hardly anything per hour. To make that mental shift, to all of a sudden, to demand premium prices, that was the big turning point, and I suppose, the biggest turning point in the business because without that, the business probably wouldn't still be here. Yeah, the mental shift was the biggest, and the mental shift came from speaking to a coach. It didn't come internally. It come from getting someone else's perspective and someone else's help, which, I suppose, links back to investing in yourself.

Paul: Just on that, did you just charge more? I know when we sort of hit that realisation, I literally doubled our prices overnight, and nothing happened, in the fact that we still got people coming in, none of our existing clients dropped off. It was a real lesson for me - just because someone had said you should charge more, and I just bit the bullet one day and just doubled it.

Oli: So, essentially, yeah, you should charge more. What I've always done every time I've increased my prices is always keep the current customers on the same pricing structure just to make sure I'm not completely risking everything. Always calculated risks. Then any new customer that comes in, you're at this new price.

What I've always found is when you increase your prices, you naturally step your game up in terms of how you think about yourself, how you position yourself, your quality of marketing, the quality of service. Everything steps up without any real thought behind it. It just naturally happens. So, yeah, just do it, I think, is the best approach. Everything else naturally follows.

Paul: So that leads to the last ditch question. Is there a bit of advice that you would give to those business owners that are not quite hitting their mark?

Oli: Perfect. So I suppose the biggest thing that made the biggest difference, to give some advice, would be to go back to basics. I think we get completely mottled up at the moment. We look at our competitors, and we take a bit of what they're offering, and you see other people that you think are doing well, or they may be doing well, and you try and replicate them, and you come up with some weird offering most of the time. All you need to do is go back to basics and think, "What's the best way to help this client in need?"

And if you go back to basics, it becomes really easy, and it's a real easy thing to sell. It's a real easy thing for them to buy. But when he comes in with silly consulting offers, where you got a little bit of this, but not a little bit of that, and it all gets a little bit confusing, then it proves difficult to sell. But really simple, done for you, done with you offerings that are more basic, easier for the prospect to buy and easier for you to sell. So going back to basics would be the biggest bit of advice I'd give.

Don't get too close

Don't get too close

This is a difficult one, both to talk about succinctly and also to really take heed of. But as a business owner it is really important to see your business a tool not the 'end purpose'.

There are very few, if any, business owners who go into business JUST to be a business owner. They go into it because they believe it can facilitate the type of lifestyle that they want. But it is really easy to forget that and start to get too close.

All business owners are, almost by definition emotionally invested in their business. It's a physical manifestation of their beliefs drive and hard work but if you get too close to your business and forget WHY it is actually there, it is all too easy to start making bad decisions.

We see a lot of people who have almost been 'sucked into' living someone else's business dream. They are working longer hours trying to earn more money but never seeing their families or friends and crucially they aren't enjoying it or getting what they wanted from it.

The typical example of this is when you meet another business owner and they relish telling you – almost as if it's a badge of honor - that they haven't had a holiday in 6 months. WHY?!

What's the point of running a business if it isn't delivering you a good lifestyle? If it is holiday that you really want, get a job they'll actually pay you to be on holiday!!

It's really tough to do though because in many cases the fact that you do care is what drives you forward especially through difficult times - you want it to succeed. But if you start making decisions for the wrong reasons then you will end up working really hard for something you don't truly want.

So you need a plan and a really smart place to start is sit down with a financial advisor and work through the numbers of what you need and want to sustain your lifestyle. You can then work back, make the right decisions and take the right actions that are going to make that happen.

Then you need to regularly check what you are doing against where you want to get to. A great way of doing this (and we've spoke about this before) is surround yourself with the right people. People who get it, they know what it is like to be a driven business owner, and they are walking the walk. Having easy and regular access to these kind of people is critical as they will be able to keep you on track, keep you motivated and inspired... and pull you back if necessary.

The reality is people like that are rarer than you think – most business owners just kid themselves. In essence what they have actually created is a poorly paid job they are trapped in the day to day working for their business, not the other way round. Classic examples that are too close to their business not the end goal.

Just because you are a business owner does not mean you have to be a millionaire. Your business is about the most personal thing in your life – it only needs to deliver what YOU want it to whether that is more money or more time – or both

So be proud of your businesses output, be respectful of what it can achieve but don't forget why it is there – and Who works for Who!

Book bonus available here:
www.marketingjumpleads.com/game-changer-book-bonuses

Its all about amplification

Its all about amplification

Most businesses want to grow, they want to be bigger, whether it be for financial gain or to give them the ability to work less. For this to happen they need to bring in a steady stream of new customers and improve the frequency of purchase from existing customers.

It's a universal truth that as a business there is no standing still. If you are not growing you ARE shrinking – customers will always leave, costs will always go up – you are always going to need to attract new customers...

No businesses have ever 100% failed in marketing – so there is always something that has driven results, whether it be a "piece of marketing" or pounding the streets. So when you do find something that works – do more of it.

Now that might sound alarmingly simple...and it is. But we are always surprised at just how many business owners find a piece of marketing that has brought results but they have neither tried it again nor tried to do it on a bigger scale.

Marketing is not an exact science, it's a series of tests. There are no silver bullets and so when you do find something that works you need to keep doing it and the smart money is on doing it on a bigger scale – you amplify it.

More than ever before, you can track how well each piece of your marketing is working. So it is easy to get a clear picture of what is your most profitable marketing activity and what hasn't worked as well and as such needs tweaking (or ditching). Once you start to think this way, you can make decisions based on facts not hunches and be very clear on where you need to direct more of your marketing spend.

So if every time you drop 1000 flyers out you get 10 new clients what about dropping 2000 out? Or if for every £100 you are spending on Facebook ads you are getting £200 back how can you spend more? Yes these are simplistic examples but the thinking is clear.

Again it seems really obvious but for many businesses Amplification just isn't on their radar. Instead they seem to approach marketing as a 'binge'. They do some marketing, it works or it doesn't, they stop for a bit and then try something else.

It goes without saying that marketing needs to be a constant – even if you think you have got al the customers you can handle.

So get close to your numbers, work out what your most successful marketing activity is and how you can make it bigger and better.

You have enough to do without having to start every time from a blank piece of paper. So don't ignore what you've already tried, just make it bigger.

Book bonus available here:
www.marketingjumpleads.com/game-changer-book-bonuses

Pictures can build profits

Pictures can build profits

Marketing is about reaching potential customers to invoke a change in their behaviour, giving them a reason to act. The only way to truly make that shift in perception is to be where people are engaging and spending time. And Instagram is where your potential new customers are doing just that.

Instagram offers such a unique level of engagement for individuals and brands alike.

IT'S OVERWHELMINGINLY MOBILE

Instagram is one of the few social networks that lives almost entirely in your pocket. Or at least on a touchscreen. This makes it a highly personal experience, and a product entirely of the mobile Internet. As such, it provides unique access to the sought after mobile audience, and is so easy and elegant when on the go, that its users are highly active.

IT'S (Mostly) JUST VISUALS

There's not a whole lot you can post other than pictures, short videos, and a few words. You can get creative and turn pictures into blocks of text, and the comment sections certainly take on lives of their own, but Instagram limits what elements you can include in your posts. This gets back to its elegance and simplicity that has made it so popular among mobile users. It is the killer app when it comes to sharing images, and casts aside the clutter that distracts users' attention and patience in most social networks.

NO LINKS

Aside from sponsored posts (which are currently pretty sparse), Instagram is remarkably non-spammy. Other than one link in your profile bio, there are no hyperlinks allowed. This presents a challenge but also an opportunity for sincere engagement and sharing. Instagram is decidedly not intended as a tool to rack up clicks which helps it feel more genuine.

All of this makes Instagram a more purely enjoyable and intimate platform, and a prime space for making connections and drawing personal engagement. By extension, generating brand awareness and engaging with your audience through a powerful image-led presence— despite the utter lack of links, buttons, popups, etc.—can drive more leads and increases sales and sign-ups.

Use the power of Instagram to drive users to your site and build your network

Instagram provides a platform for creating and sharing the visual aspects of your business, acting as a portal into the mission and ethos of your brand, and further defining the message you otherwise deliver in blog posts, podcasts and other content efforts.

It also allows more of a personal touch than most other platforms, sharing images as miniature stories from behind the scenes of your business. It is a personal, visual representation of your business delivered and consumed in real time. As a growth tool, Instagram can be effective across a variety of industries.

Pictures really can build profits

Facebook bought Instagram for 1 billion dollars in April 2012. Why?

Because it wanted to buy soul. The users of Instagram are still enamoured with their app, so much so that they were outraged by the sale.

"Facebook bought the thing that is hardest to fake. It bought sincerity," says Paul Ford at NY Mag.

The link of these two mighty platforms brings new and exciting opportunities for your business.

Book bonus available here:
www.marketingjumpleads.com/game-changer-book-bonuses

Paul Chapman *MarketingJumpleads*

Paul is a Speaker, creative thinker and Strategist. A true ideas machine and has the unique ability to find the solution that works that no-one has thought about yet. Alongside his business partner Julia they run Marketing Jumpleads, a Midlands based agency focussing on helping business get their marketing done.
www.marketingjumpleads.com

Julia: So the answers could be interesting here ... business partner! Why are you a business owner, an entrepreneur, rather than being employed? What's it for you?

Paul: In the old days, I had a great job, a job I loved, for a long time, and it paid me well, and I learned a massive, massive amount. But it just got to a stage where, rightly or wrongly, I wasn't enjoying it anymore. I think a lot of it was because I wanted to do things differently.

I didn't feel the limited skills I had were being used properly. And I am not be self depreciating here, I know what I'm good at, and I know what I'm not good at, and I didn't think I was doing the best possible thing, that my skills would allow for the clients and it was weighing on my mind.

I wasn't enjoying it because I wasn't doing the stuff I love, and I felt I could have done something different that I had proved over and again was useful to the business and the clients, the stuff I was doing meant that I wasn't giving the best with what I've got available to the people I was trying to help. – Not sure if that makes sense?

So there was that nagging away at me plus it came at a time where a lot was changing for me family wise. And I just decided if I believed they should be used. So I, literally, quit working and had a baby and bought a big house all at the same time, which I'm not necessarily sure is to be recommended.

But I think mainly it was that sort of feeling that I'm not giving my everything because I'm not doing the right stuff, tied in with the need for more freedom.

I loved my job. I got paid nicely for it. But I could easily be in the office 7:30, leaving the office at 6:30, 7:30, and going home, kind of thinking, stressing about it all night. I don't want to do that any more.

When we were growing up, I couldn't tell you what my old man earned. I don't think we were overly wealthy but I have no complaints I had a fabulous childhood, but I do know he came to all my schiool plays. I know he came to all my rugby games. He came to my hockey games. That's what I remember, my dad being there. And that is exactly what I want to do for my boys. That freedom thing is massive for me.

That's the biggest thing, I think, for me about running a business is the fact that I get to choose everything. I choose who I work for, who I don't work for, which I think a lot of business owners forget. I choose what I earn. Again, I think a lot of people forget that. Lots of people kind of think, well, no one will pay me more, which is just nonsense. Some people will pay a thousand for a cup and some people will pay a tenner for a cup. You choose, you pick it.

So I think, in general, I look at it all and it comes down to freedom. I can do what I want, when I want, with who I want, and take the time off I want. If I want to stop today and do nothing, that's what I'll do. I'll go out and play with the kids or whatever it is.

So the lifestyle is crucial but so is the money. I earn more now I run a business than I did in employment and for me that is a big part of it too.

There's lots of people out there that say it's not all about the money stuff, and I get that, and I do agree to some level. But life can be quite difficult without money. We have a lovely lifestyle. I want to keep that lifestyle. I'd like to improve on it. I know I don't desire to be a millionaire, it's not what I am working for, more of a happy byproduct, but it's not really why I'm doing this. This is about giving me a lifestyle that I want and providing a lifestyle for my family, which involves me being able to enjoy it

I think lots of people end up running a business, but doing it for someone else's business dream. Your business is about the most personal thing you can have because you only need it to deliver what you and your family want. If you want it to deliver 20 grand a year in 10 days' work, that's possible. If you want to deliver 20 million, you've got to do different things, and you probably got to put more time in it. We know lots of business owners that are earning much less than they could, but that's what they want it to do. I think that's the beauty of your business. It is that freedom to deliver exactly what you want, regardless of what everyone else thinks it should deliver.

Julia: So success is not a figure, it's not a financial figure necessarily. It's other stuff. And people forget that sometimes.

Paul: Yes I've got figures that I want to earn now. I've got figures that I contribute to my future pot. That needs to be there. You have to have a firm grasp on what you want to earn, what you need to earn to achieve your lifestyle because otherwise you don't know if you are getting closer to the goal or further away. When I first started I charged £60 an hour because I thought it would be funny to paid by the minute. Literally, that was my thinking.

It wasn't until I went and did some maths, and did the equation that I think we've spoken about before (that is also in the book) and worked out I needed to be charging more than that. So whilst I think I'm really successful, I'm doing really well and I'm filling my diary, every hour I sell at £60 is actually taking me further away from where I want to get to, not towards it.

So you do need to know that sort of figures, and the financial stuff is important, but realistically, it's freedom. I can do what I want, when I want. We could, you and I, stop working for a couple of months, and conceivably, not a lot would change. It's not a smart thing to do, and we are probably not there yet. But that kind of freedom is a big part of it.

Julia: So in a way, you've answered it but what does success look like?

Paul: I don't have a particularly extravagant lifestyle. I like what I like. I'm not very good with money. It's something that causes me stress. It's just how I think. I can write words, see marketing strategies, and come up with ideas that just work, but figures don't sit well. So I just don't want to worry about it. That's my thing. I don't want to worry about money. That's not all about becoming a millionaire, its knowing what I need to have the life I want and not having to worry about not having enough.

I know I can buy whatever I want, again, that's not flashy, I don't desire very expensive things. It's knowing that I've prepared a life and I can give my kids the best possible things. Again, as kids we were very lucky. If there was school trips, the answer was yes. Mum and Dad found a way to send my brother and I away, as and when they came up. And I want to be able to do the same.

That financial bit is there, but success is really when I can entirely do what I want. And the reality is at the moment I am not there. Could I take two years off? Possibly, but probably not, that's probably too long. But we will get to a point where I do have that absolutely entire freedom.

I think a lot of is, also, is that I can go and learn something new, go and do something new. Obviously this is a bit weird because you're interviewing me and we've got two or three businesses going on. I quite like the idea doing something completely different, I don't know, sell T-shirts or something, that kind of thing, where I can keep that spark of creativity that I think is in there somewhere. I can direct it to other stuff. Having a business that allows you to do that. That's it, for me, I think.

Julia: Whilst we are not able to take a couple of years off yet you are doing pretty well – why do you think that is?

Paul: I don't see me as having done well yet. I think we're on the right track and we've done all right. But I think the secret for me is that I do what I am good at.

I'm good at so few things, and, again, it's like I'm being all coy or whatever here, but really I'm not - there's a lot of stuff that me touching in the business will be detrimental because I'm not good at it. It takes too long, it causes stress, which means actually the time, and the energy, and the head space, and the clear head space for the stuff I'm good at becomes less and less. I think it is me doing the thing that I'm good at as often as possible is why we are doing so well and I don't take all credit for that. I mean, far, far, far from it. The business wouldn't work without the stuff you do and our team does, but I think, too often, business owners are doing the wrong stuff, stuff they're not good at, which is they don't enjoy it, it takes too long, and it's costing money.

Julia: Yes often they mess about on the stuff that they are not good at and it just frustrates and wastes time and money. So then, that leads on nicely, why do you think most business owners struggle or fail?

Paul: I think it's because they take a lot of time to do stuff. I think people are very good at getting ready. I think there is a romance about business as well, and people look at business owners, particularly successful business owners and think it's easy. The truth is successful business owners make it look easy because they've got a lot of stuff going on, and they've got steps, and they've got strategies. They've got all that kind of stuff, but only because they've worked their absolutely nuts off to get there. It's often a serious of pretty mundane steps that lead to the spectacular results

I think lots of people, get into business, and if I am honest they are not cut out for it. Let me be really careful here because not for a second am I saying business owners are cooler, better, more noble, that's not true. It's just a different route. And like anything some people are suited to it, some people aren't.

I do, genuinely, think lots of people who end up running a business because they think it's a cool thing to do, just shouldn't be. Again, we see it a lot when we're out at meeting people, and you said it yourself, it's like a badge of honor. People are telling me, "Oh, I work so hard, I haven't taken a holiday in six months." I'm like, "What's the point? Go and get a job. They'll pay you to have holiday. You actually get days where you can be on a beach, and they are paying you money."

Again, because I don't want to come across as saying being a business owner is better, but this is why, as I said earlier, it has to be the most personal thing. Because if your measure of success and, vice versa, the thing that's bad about your world is your holidays, well, go and find something that enables you to do that.

A lot of us aren't good business owners. Lots of people aren't cut out to be business owners. Lots of people shouldn't do it. They shouldn't see that as a bad thing or as a failure. The only thing that I give any kind of hoots about is wife and family. If what I'm doing isn't making their our collective life better then I'll do a different stuff.

If I, genuinely and truthfully, believed I would have a better life for me, my wife and family by having a job, I'd have a job. But my measure of success involve me spending time whenever I want to with them and that is something very difficult to do when you have a job.

Julia: So if you were starting again then, if you're going right back to day one, what's the one thing you wish you had known? What's the missing ingredient?

Paul: I'd like to have given myself more confidence of what was possible, I think. Looking back though it is so difficult because when I started in business the bulk of those first couple of years because of new babies I had literally no sleep for nearly 2 years and that isn't conducive to feeling confident and to making good decisions that help build confidence...

So I think just reminding yourself it is possible. Running a business is hard, when you start, particularly if you're not naturally good at lots of things. When you have a small thing that you do very well, that's great, but there's a lot to worry about. And I think this is particularly the case when you have come from being employed with a team around you to do the stuff.

So what do I wish I'd known? I wish I'd learned more quicker. I do wish I'd learned more. I think I know lots of stuff, but I wish I'd learned quicker.

I wish I'd invested in people quicker.. Again, I think you mentioned it earlier. It's that kind of false economy of I'll do it, but actually I'm spending a lot of time just not doing the stuff that actually ,makes sure I get paid. I read a book recently, and it posed the questions "what is the one thing that each and every person in that business should be doing to get the business forward?" I think that too many business owners hold onto too much stuff. Guys that are good at sales doing their own accounts – it'll take then 4 times as long and chances are their charge out rate will be much higher than their bookkeepers, so doing the books themselves is actually costing them money.

Julia: And I think, also we're not good at actually congratulating ourselves. No one ever says, "Well, done as a business owner" even though you are keeping it all afloat yourself, but you always think, "I haven't done this," and you focus on what you haven't done rather than saying, "Well done, I have actually achieved all this."

Paul: And that's really interesting. It is so easy to forget how far we've come. My wife is brilliant. I'll come home in stress that we are not moving fast enough, and she'll come and point to our lifestyle and happy kids and holidays, that sort of thing. I think that's just a business owner thing. I think we're more likely to be more self-deprecating than we are self-congratulation. I think -- sorry -- which is probably a long-winded answer to the question -

While I'm at it...another big thing, I wish I'd spent more time with the right people.

I think that's something I wish I'd known then that, actually, you can get so much value just from being with other people, but the difficulty then is finding those other people. They don't normally hang out at networking groups. They're often not family. They're often not the people closest to you because it's different running a business and it's hard to know what it's like if you don't do it.

Julia: So what, then, do you think has been the most potent strategy for the business you got today?

Paul: For me, I go meet people. Overwhelming, that's the thing I do. I'll go meet people. Oddly, they seem to like me, which I still find very, very peculiar.

It's an interesting time to be in business at the moment, we have got the best opportunities we've ever had to find new business, things like Facebook and it ability to accurately target people. The minutia of detail we can find about our prospects and thus have the ability to speak directly to them is beyond anything we've had before.

The downside of that is lots more people are using these tools. Lots more people are trying it. So it's easy to disappear into the noise.

This is why the face to face stuff is so important. As the world gets more technologically advanced and used to doing everything automatically, there's still an enormous place for someone that will sit and talk to you face to face, and just be nice. It's like the networking principle no one likes that guy that just comes up and tries to sell you stuff. But if you just talk, listen, try and help and "entertain" it makes a real difference.

Form relationships, and yes of course you should be forming relationships online but don't forget the power of actually meeting with people. It's the same with the phone - it gets forgotten a lot, but it works, just pick up and call. Say, "Hey, look, I just saw this. Don't know if there's any interest. Is it worth a chat?" And often that way people will say, "Yeah. Great." Then it's just go and be nice, useful, helpful, all the normal stuff.

Julia: Yeah. I think in this whole digital world we've almost forgotten the whole proper human contact bit.

Paul: Yeah, absolutely.

Julia: It's as important now as it's ever been really.

Paul: I think, as a side issue, lots of businesses aren't good at that, but that can't be an excuse. Find someone to do it. I can think of a particular business where they're just unpleasant, and unfriendly, and difficult to deal with, and that's just because that's how the guy is. That's kind of not his fault, really. That's just how he is.

If that's the way you are, look, chin up, that's the way it is. Find someone else to handle that first phone call. It's easy and cheap to do. You can outsource. You could train yourself but chances are if it's not your thing it's never going to be natural. And this is where you have to think as a business owner, and have a good look at what do people see when they look at my business I think it's something a lot of guys forget about.

Julia: So no regrets then, running own your own business?

Paul: Oh, God, no. No, no, no, no. I'd do it in a heartbeat. I'm very lucky that you and I sort of found each other, and we have such similar ethic, outlook thoughts and vision and kind of a commitment to what we think is the most helpful thing we can do.

But, no, I love doing it. I mean, you have those days where you think, "I wonder if there's any jobs at Tesco today?" I love what I do. I love it, genuinely.

The thing I get the most passion from is actually helping, seeing business owners grow and do stuff. That's great that I get to do that as a job. So, no, I mean, I'm sure there's things I wish I'd done differently, but I love it. I love it for what I do and I love it for what it gives me. I'm seeing kids grow up and spending time with wife, and have a bit of time for myself, and fitness and that. All the things that the business contributes to my life. It doesn't take it away. I mean, yeah, we all have days where we'll not see daylight, and we'll just work and work, and that's fine. That's the other side of the coin. But no, no regrets. I'd do it again in a heartbeat.

Take the time out between thinking and action

Take the time out between thinking and action

Thinking regularly and deeply is critical to your business' success and the majority of business owners don't do it anywhere near as much as they should. Having said that, thinking on it's own won't make you rich. Action makes you successful.

Almost all business owners have thoughts and plans, ideas that they believe will move their business forward but they very rarely see the light of day, because they stay on the drawing board for a long, long time.

If you look at all the successful business people, and we are not just talking the Branson's of this world – it's the same for all the successful local businesses around - they have something in common.

They think and they act – almost as one motion.

This is hugely important, and if you can **cut the time between the thought and the action,** three key things will happen:

1) You business will move forward. There is no substitute for activity, and it's a cast iron guarantee that your business will not grow through thought alone.

2) You will learn more - and become more successful. As Geoffrey Boycott may have said, *"you can't learn about cricket by sitting in the stands – you need to play"* and it's the same in business. You will learn so much more by making the idea live, about what works, what won't and what you can do next time - than you ever could just by running scenarios in your mind

3) You'll feel better – for many people stress in business come from the feeling of futility. That feeling that everything is happening to them and they can't do anything about it. If you start to try things, take action almost regardless of the result, you tend to feel more in control...and you are more likely to keep going.

If it's the fear of failure that is stopping you, we can help there too. You will fail.

Marketing, and (dare we say it) most of business is a series of tests. There are very few guarantees and even fewer silver bullets, you just have to think carefully about what you feel is the best route and give it a go. The reality is you can't find out what will work without giving it a go.

Go on, try it, we dare you...

Game Changer Thirty Five

You need a team...

You need a team...

There is an ancient Chinese proverb that goes.

Go fast - go alone
Go far travel together

It's bang on! Too many business owners are trying to get it all done by themselves and it's not just crazy – it's impossible. If you aspire to build a big business or a business that allows you complete freedom over how much time you spend in it, you need to have people around you. Not just for support, but to actually get the stuff done that goes hand in hand with success.

One of the really interesting things that have come out of the interviews for this book is that almost all the business owners talk about the importance of their team either employed or 'out-sourced' and many talking about how they wish they had built a team sooner.

To truly build a bigger and importantly sustainable business you need people to do some of the work. Whilst I am sure there are a few examples out there of people doing it solo, the overwhelming numbers of successful business are not run by and were not grown by, just one person.

We are not necessarily talking about employing people, although for many people having full time support is the right answer – this could just be having a team of outsource skills at your finger tips to make stuff happen.

Either way if you try and get it all done alone your will SERIOUSLY stunt your ability to grow. We mean this in both how much physically you can get done in 24 hours but also your headspace to come up with the ongoing plan.

This is a BIG step for many entrepreneurs especially because pretty much by definition they set up on their own and do everything from day one themselves. But it's an important one and it should be embraced sooner rather than later.

Where to start?

Write a list of everything you do in your business from admin and accounts to sales and marketing.

Next start to put some numbers on it. If you haven't done already run the equation earlier on in the book and get clear what your time "costs you." Then go through and put a time against all the jobs you do right now.

Look at which bits **only you** can do and be ruthless. This isn't what other people won't be able to do as well as you – it is what can only you do.

Then look at the maths. The reality is, even before you get to a skill level, on a purely cost versus reward level there are a lot of things that you should not be doing in your business.

Think about it, if you are doing your own accounts each month and your cost per hour is anything more than a good book keeper (£10 - £20) per hour you are wasting your money and your time. Factor in the fact that they will likely do it quicker and better than you – the picture starts to make sense.

The over arching response we hear when we speak about this with new clients is that they say they can't afford to have someone take some of the work – but the reality is if they are serious about growing a business and not having it entirely dependent on them until they retire – they can't afford NOT to get help.

It simply won't all happen if you do it on your own.

Book bonus available here:
www.marketingjumpleads.com/game-changer-book-bonuses

Capturing it live

Capturing it live

"People love the novelty of viewing someone in a live moment when anything could happen. It's the new reality TV" Hubspot

Facebook is accelerating quickly into the world of live streaming, now making it possible for all of the site's users to broadcast videos of almost anything to a huge audience.

Facebook's massive global reach brings the technology to a bigger audience than ever. The feature was first announced in 2015 and was available only to celebrities. Since then, Facebook has made it available to any user with an active profile or Page.

Why is this a game changer? Because it's an awesome way to use the power of live video to communicate brand stories and build authentic, intimate relationships with fans and followers.

The people dominating live video on Facebook at the moment are big media companies or celebrities - but there's no reason you or your business couldn't become video famous using this powerful medium. SME's are quickly catching on to the possibilities.

We've always stress the importance of video as part of your marketing mix. Facebook adding live steaming has raised that importance to a whole new level. You used to need expensive desktop equipment to be streaming live...it is now accessible to everyone and anyone.

It's easy to do, quick, instant and the curiosity gene of your audience pulls them to your stream in big numbers and at engagement levels you won't have enjoyed before. There are incredible adoption and engagement levels with this new format. It's exciting for anyone running marketing campaigns!

Facebook are wholeheartedly behind their live streaming options. That's worth remembering.

Simply put **Facebook ranks FB Live videos higher than other videos and other types of posts,** so we recommend spacing out your Facebook Live videos with other Facebook content you post.

Right now your organic (non-paid for) reach with live streaming will put all your other Facebook updates in the shade.

Facebook Live broadcasts may seem intimidating at first, but there's an easy solution. Create a plan and end goal to get your first live stream done. When you see a purpose that will result in expanding your business, client base, and bottom line, Facebook Live broadcasts are a lot easier to tackle!

Try something simple. Make the leap.

Live video is only going to get bigger as time goes on, so expect to see more and more streams appearing on your feed. You and your business need to be there too.

Book bonus available here:
www.marketingjumpleads.com/game-changer-book-bonuses

Simon Lyons *Version 22*

Version 22 is a design studio that creates innovative products that solve the everyday problems around the home in ways that make you smile. Simon founded Version 22 back in 2012 whilst still at university as a means of making his ideas a reality. To date Version 22's two current products Geco Hub and Nimble have won multiple national awards, raised tens of thousands of pounds in crowdfunded sales and sold to over 60 countries. They've even shown up in The Sunday Times and The Economist too!

www.version22.com

Paul: What's it really about for you? Why are you doing what you are currently doing rather than having a job working for someone else? What's led you to where you are now?

Simon: Well, it's a few reasons. It's an outlet for my ideas. So I've always liked designing and creating things. I always thought, when I was growing up, the best way to create my own ideas was to go work for someone else. Go work for a big design firm, and then slowly build up a bit of influence, and get a managerial position, and be able to then decide what gets made. I figured out, well actually, if I go it alone, it's a bit of risk there and a lot more work, but I get to make my own things straightaway. So that was one. To be honest, I want the freedom of location and time, so to be able to base myself anywhere, and work whichever days of the week I want to, and that sort of thing. So, ultimately, it means more work upfront, but then more freedom down the line.

Paul: What does success look like for you? How do you know it's worth the hassle?

Simon: To me, that's when the business will run without my day-to-day presence. So I could up and leave for three weeks and go to another country and the business would still tick. There would still be clients coming in, there'd still be goods being sold, there'd still be products being shipped out. Marketing would still be going out there. Just having things taken care of without me and reaching a point where I'm able to pay myself enough to not have to worry about money. So I'm not talking tens of millions, but enough to be able to live a good life. But, more importantly, have the hours to actually live it. So rather than working 70-80 hour weeks, being able to cut it down to almost a part-time thing would be brilliant.

Paul: It sort of hit me with age really, I was working incredibly hard for someone else. I loved it, but I never had any time. I was always working. I never had any off time. n I was totally immersed in their business and doing my bit to make it the best I could. The pay was good but I never got to enjoy it.

Simon: No, definitely. Definitely. I think I'd definitely be happier working half the hours for half the money than double the hours for five times the money or whatever it is.

Paul: Yeah. I understand that, mate. So I think, looking at all the stuff you've achieved over the last couple of years, it is pretty special. Why do you think you have done so well?

Simon: I'm not sure really. I think I'm passionate about what I'm doing. I think that's important. If the passion's not there, then you're not going to put in the extra hours and bounce back from all of the failures that you're going to have. So you need to be passionate about what you're doing and, also, I'm constantly trying to do things that make me uncomfortable.

Simon: So situations that at one time I would immediately have said "no" to, I try and force myself to do them. I used to not like pitching. I used to not like being on video. I used to not like networking. All that sort of stuff. But one at a time, just tackling them head-on and just doing them anyway. Suddenly, it becomes a new norm and then there's another challenge to tackle ahead of that.

Paul: That's really interesting, that sort of pushing yourself out to stuff that you know has to be done, but never yet done. Probably on the same lines, why do you think then that most business owners arguably struggle or fail?

Simon: I think they fail in the sense that the business stops functioning and goes out of business or whatever because they're afraid of failing. So, if you're taking the risks, and trying new things, and putting yourself out of the comfort zone, then you'll get it wrong more times than you get it right, but at least you'll get some things right. Whereas, if you just stick with what you know, then it might work for a short time. But, slowly and surely, it'll either stagnate or decline. Then, you're stuck with a business that's not working anymore. So I think that's the main thing. Even if you are afraid, just doing it anyway and just having a go because you're not going to die if your business fails. If you play it too safe, then obviously there is such thing as taking too much risk. But, if you play it too safe, that's just as bad.

Paul: So many people out there aren't willing to do the stuff that no one else will.

There are two business owners out there inventing products and both are thinking, "I don't like being on video." One of them is thinking, "I don't like being on video. And the other is thinking I don't like being on video but I know I can grow my business with it. I'll suck it up and get on with it." That's a big difference.

Simon: No, definitely. And not necessarily doing what everyone else is doing, so being on the new social networks before anyone else because, yes, they might not catch on. They might be a big thing. But it's a bit of a line grab. You can advertise for much less. You can have a larger reach earlier on. There's so many benefits to going at it first. So, yeah, there's going to be risks. So they might fall flat on their face and not make it past a couple of years. But some of them might grow and, by the time everyone else is on that platform, you're way ahead. So that's just one example.

Paul: And along that line, is there something that you know now that you really wish you'd known or been told kind of day one, a bit of advice, an action you wished you'd taken, or something like that?

Simon: If there's one thing, it would probably be to speak to the experts. So, although you have to try and learn stuff for yourself, it's a massive shortcut if you could speak to someone who's already been and done what you're trying to achieve because so many times I've made mistakes with designing a product thinking I'm making it cheap when I'm actually making it more expensive. If I'd instead taken a sketch of a new idea to a manufacturer before I actually spent the time to CAD it up, then they would have said, "No, that's going to be more expensive when you do this." Likewise in marketing and sales, taking on people that know more than you, I think, and not being too proud to do that.

Paul: If you started again what would you do differently?

Simon: I'd say launching sooner. So learning that good is good enough because it's the same. It's a phrase thrown around a lot, but it applies to all sorts of things, our marketing campaigns, and products, and that sort of thing. The first Kickstarter campaign I did failed. But I spent months and months and months doing it, and the last month or so was just tiny, little tweaks. Then, when I launched, I found out there was something fundamentally wrong with it, which meant I had to go back to the drawing board and do another campaign. I would have learned the same thing if I'd launched a month or two months earlier. So that's a big one. Then, not overthinking social media marketing campaigns too much because, for me, I've always improved my campaigns by just launching what I've got and seeing what happens as opposed to trying to make it perfect and then launching because, both times, the first one you launch doesn't work. So it's better to launch sooner, learn, and then launch again as opposed to spending all that time developing the first try.

Paul: You mentioned a bit of social media. Has there been a marketing strategy, a business strategy, that you'd say, "That's been one of the most potent. Doing X has brought me more momentum than anything else."?

Simon: In terms of list building, competitions have been the best for me, running social media competitions and getting email signups that way. In terms of making sales, cross promotions have been the best for me. So with my crowd-funding campaign, I would recommend other crowd-funding campaigns and they would do the same in return. That had, by far, the best ROI because it was free for both of us to implement and we both made direct sales off the back of it. So there's no sales funnel. It was straight to a sales page and it worked brilliantly.

Paul: Ace. Last question: if you were going to give a business owner a bit of advice, what would be the biggest thing?

Simon: Not being afraid to work together with people in a similar market as you, whether that's for cross promotion, advice, sharing contacts, sharing things you've learned, that sort of thing. Just because you're in the same market, it doesn't mean you're competing with each other. That's one thing that I've done that's helped with the cross promotion side of things with new contacts for potential customers, with trade shows, with being put in touch with certain people with certain expertise. A lot of that has come through just building a network of people in a similar market to mine.

Paul: Interesting. Again, it's one of those things that I suppose it goes back to experience really in the fact that, once you get a bit further down the line, you have the experience to realise that you can work very closely with some very similar businesses and all your clients aren't going to disappear to someone else.

Simon: No. So companies that have the same customers, but not necessarily the same offering, that's what I mean. So, if you're both appealing to the same customers, but not competing in what you're offering them, then you've got nothing to lose and everything to gain by partnering with people like that.

Perfection is overrated

Perfection is overrated

One of the enemies of entrepreneurs is the pursuit of perfection. The endless fine tuning, tweaking and procrastinating putting off actually getting that letter posted, that email campaign sent or those calls made.

The ability to let it go and the belief that good really is good enough can be so hard. We all have those projects that are never quite finished. Ideas and campaigns you've never quite been happy about, that sit in your inbox or collect dust on a shelf.

Please step away from this thinking, leave perfection to surgeons, and just 'get it out there'. Taking action and implementation is how you move your business forward and achieve important speed to make breakthroughs.

Get your idea out there...see if you get some traction. If it takes off then you can tweak and improve. One of Dan Kennedy's key sayings is "You don't have to get it right, you have to get it going".

An email campaign with the odd typo that is sent will give you way better returns than the perfect email campaign that never goes out. The leaflet with a small spelling mistake can be handed out and working for your business or you can being sending proofs back and forth with your printer for weeks and miss opportunities.

Any of you that has ever used Microsoft Windows can attest to this. The earlier versions of the operating system were rife with problems but they went on to globally monopolise PC software. Microsoft didn't hold back the release of Windows until it was perfect (it still isn't!) they just sorted issues as they arose.

We are no advocating shoddy or poor work...but once you have checked a piece, pop it in envelope or hit send. You will get through sooo much more and you will quickly see what is working.

If you've been stalling in your business because of perfectionism, take action today and concentrate more on implementation. Tweak later.

Book bonus available here:
www.marketingjumpleads.com/game-changer-book-bonuses

Printed in Great Britain
by Amazon